Henry Morgan was ordained into the
in both inner-city and suburban pari
parish ministry in 1992 to set up the ⸺⸺⸺, which
supports and encourages the ministry of spiritual direction. He is
the current Chair of Spiritual Directors in Europe.

Roy Gregory has been a professional engineer and church pastor
for over 35 years. He has taught in higher education at all levels,
and has also been involved in training staff. He is a Free Church
pastor, an Open University associate lecturer, Staff Tutor at the
St Albans Centre for Christian Studies and a member of the
Annunciation Trust.

THE GOD YOU ALREADY KNOW

Developing your spiritual and prayer life

Henry Morgan and Roy Gregory

First published in Great Britain in 2009

Society for Promoting Christian Knowledge
36 Causton Street
London SW1P 4ST

The author and publisher have made every effort to ensure that the
external website and email addresses included in this book are correct and
up to date at the time of going to press. The author and publisher are not
responsible for the content, quality or continuing accessibility of the sites.

British Library Cataloguing-in-Publication Data
A catalogue record for this book is available from the British Library

ISBN 978–0–281–06155–6

1 3 5 7 9 10 8 6 4 2

Typeset by Graphicraft Ltd, Hong Kong
Printed in Great Britain by Ashford Colour Press

Produced on paper from sustainable forests

*To colleagues and friends
in Soul Space at the
Greenbelt Festival*

Contents

Contents

Part 2
DEVELOPING YOUR PRAYER LIFE

Contents

Part 4
OVER TO YOU

Editors' introduction

Beginnings

This book came out of the experience of the two of us working together in 'Soul Space', a part of the Greenbelt Festival, which has been held each year since 1973 at the end of August. Traditionally it has been a meeting place for Christianity and the arts, but it has grown into something much bigger than that. In the year 2000 a number of us were invited to go to the Festival in order to offer spiritual direction to *all* those present, in a venue called 'Soul Space'! This was never likely to happen, but we did see a lot of people that first weekend: many of them on the edge of the church, hanging on by their finger tips, for whom Greenbelt was 'their church'. We were moved and fascinated by the stories we heard. The following year we were there again and better prepared. In addition to offering a listening space for people wanting to talk about their faith journey, we also provided a prayer corner, where different ways into prayer could be read about and tried. Our experience was that most people defined prayer too narrowly, and then when their particular tight expression of it ran out of steam, they were left lost and bewildered. The prayer corner was packed out for much of the weekend.

We have both been involved over many years in talking to individuals about their faith and seeking to facilitate their growth. Together we must have clocked up thousands of hours of listening and talking. Henry is a Church of England priest who gave up parish work for a full-time ministry mainly in spiritual direction. Roy is a Free Church part-time pastor also involved in spiritual direction.

A number of years ago Henry edited *Approaches to Prayer* which we have found useful in Soul Space. After this became out of print we cooperated to produce an online version so that it could be accessible to a wider audience, see <www.annunciationtrust.org.uk/

approaches/>. *Approaches* is now in print again, and *The God You Already Know* is a natural follow-on with the same philosophy – that prayer is not the preserve of the especially holy or pious.

Approaches is a collection of prayer aids to help people to pray. This book goes on from there to address many of the issues that we talk about with people at Greenbelt and adds to this with contributions from others who have found ways to pray in particular situations writing about their experiences. These mini 'case studies' show how ordinary people face the human situation and how this has affected, challenged and developed their spiritual and prayer life.

So in producing this book we have been joined by many friends and people we have listened to, and we wish to acknowledge their important contribution in bringing richness and variety to our endeavours. They are listed with our thanks at the end of this introduction.

People on the edge – Soul Space and Greenbelt

The Greenbelt Festival is a place on the edge, which is why lots of people are drawn to it. It's a place where you can ask any questions you like – nothing is off-limits – and where all sorts of answers will be heard. It's an extraordinarily liberating place, and as a consequence there is a lot of new life to be found there. If you want something safer, something simpler with more security, then you will go elsewhere.

This book has arisen out of our experience of listening to people in Soul Space (and indeed elsewhere) telling the stories of their encounters with God, and of the lack of them, and asking the questions that arise from those experiences. At Soul Space we have seen at first hand a spiritual hunger that does not seem to be much met by the church structures that are currently in place.

Encouragingly, some of the things that have been important to us appear to speak to others – not to everybody, but to some. This book comes out of our growing conviction that the people who gather at Greenbelt are but the tip of an iceberg, and that maybe we have something to offer to a wider audience.

Our assumptions

Our work has led us to believe that most people know most of what they need to know about God already; they don't need new information, but they do need encouragement and confidence to trust their own instincts. We believe that God created us to pray and that therefore it is a natural activity of which we all have some experience.

We believe that if we pay attention life will teach us what else we need to know. God's creation is good, and life is basically friendly and can be trusted. We acknowledge that sometimes we get things wrong, or that bad things sometimes happen to us. But we believe that when either of those things does happen, then under God we can learn something from it and grow. In our experience, God is not a punishing God but a loving God. God's creation is basically good, and we as a part of that creation are basically good too, at least in God's eyes.

We further believe that we can for the most part trust ourselves, our deepest desires and our instincts. In principle, the task before us is not as difficult as we often fear it to be. It is not without its problems, but we are made in God's image, are usually doing better than we think, and have the capacity, under God, to do even better. For this task we need some help and a modest degree of self-discipline if we are going to be able to respond creatively to these opportunities. This is best accomplished safely with the support of a faith community that we trust and where we can be ourselves.

About this book

This book offers a wide range of material written in a variety of styles, and we have quite deliberately encouraged it to speak with differing voices. It is the coming together of the experience of a large number of people. The authors have different personalities and come from different church traditions but share a common aim and philosophy. Recognizing that we are all different and that there are many ways to God is important if we are each to discover for ourselves our own 'prayer voice'. It is equally important to remember that we each reflect some distinctive facet of God's image, and that the God we each know is one and the same God, however unlikely that may at times appear.

So this is not a book to be read straight through from cover to cover. It is a resource to 'dip into' and to take what speaks to you now. It may speak of different things at different times. Part 1 discusses some ideas about prayer and faces some of the difficult issues; Part 2 looks at the place of change in praying and finding God; Part 3 tells of the experience of many individuals and recounts their struggles with prayer in differing circumstances; and Part 4 is over to you!

In a little more detail, Chapter 1 encourages you to take a fresh look at where you are now on your spiritual journey.

Chapter 2 suggests that most of us already know most of what we need to know about God, but that that knowledge frequently gets buried and forgotten. It offers a way of bringing that wisdom back into our consciousness.

Chapter 3 looks at two New Testament stories that tell of people's religious experience and asks what we can learn from them for ourselves.

Chapter 4 goes on to explore the biblical insight that God is able to speak to us through anything, and offers some ways to reflect on your own life in such a way as to become more aware of this.

Chapter 5 tells the story of how for one particular person God suddenly went silent and missing, and suggests that such an experience is an almost inevitable part of everybody's spiritual journey at some point. What might we learn from it, how do we cope with it, and how might we prepare ourselves for its coming?

Chapter 6 then looks at the biblical tradition of a God who is silent or absent and wonders what it might teach us.

Chapter 7 talks about prayer being primarily God's activity and not ours. God is praying in us even when we are not aware of it. Our task is to try to work with God in prayer. It's not primarily down to us. And blessedly God is good at prayer!

Chapter 8 then looks in more detail at reviewing our life and choosing a structure that works for us. All the Christian traditions offer structures and lifestyles and these give us clues, but for things to last we must make the structure for our life our own and find a community of faith to help us.

Chapter 9 invites you to think about how you might begin to pray as you are, rather than as you are not.

Chapter 10 offers some specific ideas and aids to prayer you might like to try.

Chapter 11 attempts to earth all of this by inviting a number of people to reflect on everyday activities about which they are passionate. Our passions have usually got much to teach us and if we pursue them with joy they will usually lead us to God. We hope that this will encourage you to reflect in a new way on your own passions, and to recognize that God is much more present in your life already than you perhaps imagined.

Chapter 12 follows a similar pattern but here we asked people to reflect on times of pain and suffering. Chapter 13 stays with this pattern but looks at relationships and other areas of our lives.

Finally Chapter 14 looks at where you might find encouragement and support for your journey, and encourages you to take new steps, or retrace well-worn steps, to find 'space for your soul'.

We hope that with the help of this book you might discover or rediscover that you are made in the image of a God who loves you unconditionally, and that learning to trust this loving God is the way to true freedom.

Contributors

Our thanks go to Ray Wilkinson, who sowed the original seed out of which this book grew, and to the following for their contributions, willingly offered.

Annabel Barber	Paul Booth
Simon Barrow	Anna Botwright
Sue Bond	Liz Cannon

Mike Catling
Paul Cressall
Gideon van Dam
John Davies
Joanna Finegan
John Fisher
Guli Francis-Dehqani
Alison Froggatt
Sister Gabriel
Gavin
Mary Goldsmith
James Grenfell
Mike Harrison
Mary Hillard
Ian Howarth
Liz Lang
Christopher Lewis
Julian Maddock
Sue Makin

Sylvia Morgan
Bill Page
Patricia Price-Tomes
David Pullinger
Michael Rowberry
Gill Russell
Jane Russell
Stephanie Shah
Sue Shaw
Ruth Stables
Anne Strach
Lynn Terrell
Ned Townshend
Colin Travers
Paul Tudge
Hugh Valentine
Lydia Wells
Shelley Wild

Also to Anne Bennett, Christine Gregory and Sylvia Morgan, who read drafts of our text at various points and offered wise and helpful advice. The absence of too many errors is largely due to them. Any absence of true quality is entirely our responsibility!

Finally we wish to register our gratitude to all those who have been involved in the Annunciation Trust, past and present. Without the active encouragement of Trustees, colleagues and supporters none of this would have been possible.

Henry Morgan and Roy Gregory

Part 1

YOUR OWN EXPERIENCE
OF GOD

1

Stages of spiritual growth

———•◆•———

Many writers have offered models of the ways in which we grow spiritually as human beings. Most of them have valuable things to say, and not surprisingly there is a good deal of overlap between them. A model that we have often shared with people at Greenbelt is that set out by Elizabeth Liebert in her book *Changing Life Patterns: Adult Development in Spiritual Direction*. I will explain in outline what she says, because our experience from Soul Space is that many find it a liberating model.

But first it's important to remember that it is a *model*, no more than that. It is not a straitjacket or a box you have to fit into. It describes a process you may recognize, and which may offer you reassurance that the way you are on is indeed a way leading somewhere and not a dead end. It is not a process that will necessarily speak to everybody, and those to whom it does speak will not necessarily recognize all of it.

Elizabeth Liebert distinguishes three stages in our spiritual growth. The first she calls the *conformist* stage. Here the most important characteristic is the importance of belonging. Your spiritual reality is defined by the groups to which you belong. You conform in order to be able to have an identity as a member of a group, to which you commit and where you find the friends with whom you will share activities.

You want to do God's will, but someone has to tell you what it is that you have to do, so rules are important. You see any kind of spiritual teacher as an authority, an expert whom you expect to provide correct rules and answers.

You may tend to see things in black and white, and don't easily make allowances for individual differences. You may well be rather

3

judgemental. Your world is governed by 'shoulds' and 'oughts', so you can be very hard on yourself. You probably deny having any negative feelings.

You will present to others as a 'nice person' who does things right, and doesn't break the rules. My guess is that many regular churchgoers belong to this first stage.

When the conformist stage doesn't work for you any more then you may be moving to the *conscientious* stage. The change may be caused by many things. It might be that an issue arises in the church community where you take a different view from that of the leadership. It might be that something happens in your own life experience and you find that the teaching offered by the church simply doesn't fit it. You may find yourself joining other groups whose assumptions about life are different from yours and this leads you to question what you have previously accepted. It often happens to young adults on leaving home, and discovering a world outside the church community in which they grew up.

You possibly start asking questions that in the conformist stage were never asked. Or you start coming up with unacceptable answers to the questions that were being asked. You are no longer willing to take something as true just because somebody else says so. You want to discover your own answers to your own questions. You are being called to learn to trust yourself, and to discover your own relationship with God, rather than accept a relationship that somebody else tells you about.

It can be an extremely painful and lonely time. It may feel as if all the old certainty is gone and with it the faith that you once knew. It often feels as if you have somehow failed. Friends who are still in the conformist stage can be very critical and judgemental of you. They may accuse you of 'selling out', of 'backsliding'. They almost certainly don't understand where you are at. You will long to find a group who does understand, and yet this is quite likely not to happen. Indeed, in a sense it almost *can't* happen, because you are being led to do some spiritual learning for yourself and you can probably only do that on your own.

It can feel like leaving home. Meeting someone willing and able to provide a sounding board as you find and redefine your own identity can be a great help. The call is to become more self-aware, more trusting of your own insights and feelings, more able to relax and be yourself with others and before God. God will gradually reveal God-self as a truly personal God: 'my God' and not 'the God of my parents or my church', perhaps. As a consequence, prayer can now be more honest and the relationship with God more real. Other relationships will also change: as you are more real yourself, others will feel able to be more real with you in return, and friendships will deepen.

Conscientious people are usually people who care, but this usually means caring for others rather than themselves. Self-care is something you will still need to learn.

What is changing here is that you are no longer letting others tell you who you are and what you should think and do. Rather than giving your power and authority away to others, you are now ready to claim it for yourself.

This is not without its downside. Having claimed your authority to yourself can mean an excessive self-confidence in your own judgements and insights. '*I* have prayed about it and *I* have decided . . .' Other views are not welcomed or heeded.

You may also experience difficulty fitting your newly claimed self into the larger, ever-changing world. When other people or groups don't treat you as the unique individual you now know yourself to be, and fail to respect your new-found freedom, you may find their attitudes tough to deal with. You may find it hard to accept others who don't share your idealism. You may become cynical and alienating. Church membership is often difficult at this time.

Elizabeth Liebert's third stage is what she calls the *inter-individual* stage. She reckons that it is rare for people to reach this stage before mid-life. Some people never move into this stage; or their highest level of development may have some characteristics of this transition but be lacking in others.

These people have learnt to accept themselves with all their imperfections and so are also able to accept others as *they* are. You have learnt tolerance and compassion. Not all problems are solvable, but it is all right not to know; you don't have to be perfect and neither does anybody else. You are very creative when it comes to the pursuit of the spiritual life, because you can handle complexity, paradox, ambiguity and the difference between your inner and outer lives.

Recognizing the legitimacy of perspectives other than one's own can lead to interdependence with those whose values and goals may be antithetical to your own. Your goal is achieving harmony among groups and within yourself, to transcend the differences between yourself and others. These people are great reconcilers. There is a generosity of spirit about them.

Your criteria for your actions are not simply those of the church, society or family: they come from your own inner life. You have learnt to trust your own judgements, but you no longer feel the need to beat other people around the head with them. Since you have come to terms with yourself in a realistic way, you are able to be more compassionate and kind to yourself. Self-care springs from the realization that only the healthy person can help the other.

Because there is greater freedom within your inner world, elements from the unconscious emerge more readily. As a result you may be dealing with many so-called negative feelings. Previously ignored needs may surface, which have to be integrated.

Images of God are vague but intimacy with God is more available. God is now free to be God. What images you do find amenable may be those of your own creation. The images will be more felt than imagined. You can allow yourself to be guided by your unconscious world.

You need a companion as you deal with the fact that you must live within sinful structures and institutions that are at variance with your ideals. You will value a co-pilgrim who walks alongside you, sharing the challenges and delights of the journey. You are more interested in the journey than in arriving. Perhaps you need to learn to die to yourself when you accept the autonomy of others, when you build relationships that are truly mutual and intimate, and when you confront the sinful structures in which you find your life entwined.

Is Liebert's model one you recognize? There is nothing judgemental about where you feel yourself to be in these three stages.

You are where you are. In all probability you won't reckon that you are all neatly in one place: different parts of life may be at different stages of growth. Bits of life experience may suddenly catapult you forward or send you back to a place you thought you had left behind, rather like snakes and ladders! And there is nothing you can do about 'moving yourself on' to the next stage: it will happen naturally as and when you are ready for it. There is no competition here.

But the model may help you to name where you are, to accept yourself in that place, and to recognize the gifts and learning opportunities that may await you there.

My experience says that finding yourself moving from one stage to another, in one area of your life, is likely to have implications in other areas. One of the potentially trickiest examples of this is when one of a married couple leaves the conformist stage for the next part of their journey. The odds are that their partner will not make the transition at the same time, and may not make it at all. Indeed it may be that their partner is never called to make it. This may well put considerable pressure on the relationship, as a faith journey that had previously gone along in tandem pretty happily may now no longer do so. The one breaking new ground may suddenly find that their partner cannot share their excitement, and it may even feel as if they are holding it back. While the one left behind may suddenly feel that the partner they felt they knew so well has suddenly become a stranger! Relationships can and do survive this experience, and with good luck will be the stronger for it. But it may not be easy. The reality is that you don't have much control of this. If you are being led onwards then you have to proceed, although you will hopefully remain sensitive to the needs of those around you.

My guess is that many of those coming to Soul Space at Greenbelt are engaged in making the tricky transition between the first two stages of Elizabeth Liebert's model. And I reckon that there are lots of other people in that place. It's not an easy place to be, but it is one of potential growth, and you will have got there because God sees that you are ready to grow, not because you have somehow failed somewhere!

But growth is not automatic. Some people will find their way through to the next stage. Some people may stay stuck for quite a long time. Some may give up the struggle and either abandon their faith journey altogether or sink back into the conformist stage they are ready to leave, because it just seems too hard to make the change.

My guess is also that there are a lot of people who are exploring this transition time, without having gone through Elizabeth Liebert's first stage at all in any obvious way. I'm thinking here of those who have no background in any faith community, but suddenly find themselves asking these spiritual questions. These folk might have quite a hard ride, as they may have little to react against as a spur to moving on, nor any obvious faith experience on which to build. They may indeed be put off exploring faith by the noisy assertions of people from the conformist stage telling them that faith is all about believing a list of certainties which they'll tell them about, which is probably the last thing they want to hear!

Perhaps all these uncertainties and difficulties are of a purpose? Maybe they happen because at a certain stage in our spiritual development we have to break out on our own and allow ourselves to be discovered by God alone, and for us to rediscover God for what may feel like the first time. This is often not easy. But it is always possible, and maybe part of this phase of the journey is coming to trust that the God who calls us can be relied upon to provide us with what we need at the appropriate time. The challenge is in accepting that we cannot control when that time is, nor can we determine what it is that we need. Instead we are being invited to a deeper trust in a God who knows our needs and the appropriate timing better than we ever could!

HM

2

The God you already know

My own faith journey, together with listening to other people telling about theirs, has led me to two basic convictions. The first is that most of us know more about God than we give ourselves credit for. God has already told us most of what we need to know. The problem is that much of it lies buried and forgotten deep within us. We need help to bring this buried treasure to the surface and to learn to trust, value and work with it. When we do so life is transformed.

The second is that God's creation is good, and we are a part of that good creation; and so life is friendly and can be trusted. Life will teach us most of what else we need to know, if we but pay attention. I am not oblivious to humanity's failings, but reckon that we are created good, with a capacity to get it wrong, rather than created bad but sometimes get it right.

In this section I explore these two key convictions, and why and how I have come to hold them. I also suggest ways in which you can become more aware of them in your own life.

I came into Christian faith through my membership of a middle-of-the-road Anglican church in suburban London. It wasn't a church that 'pushed anything' at me very much, which often felt like a weakness when I was young because I never felt I knew my Bible as well as my more evangelical Christian friends. But as I've grown older I've come to see it as a great blessing for which I'm deeply grateful, because it allowed a much more intuitive, and for me much more natural, faith to grow. I used to go to church on a Sunday morning and then go for a walk in the nearby woods before returning home for lunch. While I walked I'd wonder which girl I'd like to go out with, and how Spurs would get on in the match on Saturday, and I'd also ask if God existed, and what life was all about. From time to time I'd talk over my thoughts on the last of these questions with the young curate at our church, and it was he who one day asked me if I'd ever thought of becoming a priest. The idea must have struck a chord within me because some years later, at the conclusion of the midnight communion at Christmas, I had a sudden conviction that priesthood was indeed what God was calling me to. If I'd been asked what I thought that becoming a priest would involve me doing, I am clear that I would have replied that I thought it would allow me paid time to walk in the woods and think about God, and that I would find myself having conversations with other people about God. Naive of me, I admit, but it's what I thought.

Many years later, when I had been ordained a Church of England priest for some time, I went through a period of deep personal crisis. From being a man who could drop off as soon as his head hit the pillow I became a man who had difficulty getting to sleep, and then woke up in the middle of the night in a cold sweat. In the middle of the night my problems always seem huge and unsolvable, and cause deep dread in my heart and soul. And night after night I was waking up feeling terrible, unable to see my way through the crisis that had enveloped me. Then one night all that changed. I woke up as usual, but felt OK. I'm sure that I stayed on the bed, but it felt as if I was held above the bed, and as sure as day, God spoke to me. I don't imagine that anyone else awake in the room would have heard anything, and the message in one sense wasn't telling me anything strikingly original, but the words of reassurance struck deep. To hear them spoken directly, person-ally to me, is a very different experience from reading them cold off the printed page. And instantly my deep sense of anxiety was taken away. The crisis took much longer to resolve itself, and there remained much pain ahead, but the deep angst was gone. I knew that God loved, accepted and trusted me, whatever. I think that God has nearly always been real for me, but I had never had an experience like that before and I was overwhelmed by it. Luckily I had a friend who confirmed my experience and encouraged me to trust it, which is what I very much wanted to do. And then, slowly, a number of other things happened and things began to fall into place.

First of all I came across the work of what was then called the Alister Hardy Research Unit. Alister Hardy was Professor of Marine Biology at Oxford until he retired in the 1960s. He set up the Unit to do scientific research into people's religious experience. He put an advertisement in the Sunday papers inviting people to write to him if 'you have ever been aware of, or influenced by, a presence or power, whether you call it God or not, which was different from your everyday self'. He was encouraged by the high level of response, and a book followed (Maxwell and Tschudin, *Seeing the Invisible*) telling some of the stories he received and distinguishing types of experience. My experience fell right into the middle of one of these types, and I realized that it was not so unusual. Indeed, surveys commissioned in Nottingham and Leeds by the Research Unit suggested that two thirds of adults questioned claim to have had an experience of this sort at some time in their lives. (To learn something more of the work of the Alister Hardy Research Unit, see David Hay, *Exploring Inner Space*, 1982.) As David Hay, a later director of the Unit, summarized in the report of a study of people's spirituality:

> National surveys had told us that about half the adult population of Britain would claim to have a spirituality that is grounded on their personal experience. In-depth work where there was time to build up trust repeatedly showed that approximately two thirds of those interviewed were prepared to acknowledge and talk about their spirituality. These figures are comparable to and in some cases higher than rates reported for the United States, which in terms of formal religious practice is a much more religious country than Britain.
>
> Those people we have spoken with in the past about such moments of spiritual or religious insight, have usually taken them to be intimations of the plausibility of the religious interpretation of life, though not necessarily of Christianity. Contrary to certain commonly held stereotypes, they are more likely than other people

11

to be psychologically well balanced and to be happy. They typically speak of one of the outcomes of their experience as an increasing desire to care for those close to them as well as a sense of responsibility for the larger community and the physical environment.

(Hay and Hunt, 2000)

Second, I saw that the Bible is full of stories of people being addressed by God. Indeed, a good description of the Bible is that it is a book that tells how God spoke to a people over a long period of time.

These two things combined took me right back to my original, naive, sense of calling to priesthood, and awakened in me the desire to be the sort of priest that I felt God originally called me to be. That meant that I would need time to take seriously these moments when God spoke to me, and I would need to try to nurture a sense of openness to this God who speaks. It also meant that I felt called to try to support and encourage others who have had similar experiences.

Third, I read *The Historical Figure of Jesus* by E. P. Sanders, a leading New Testament theologian. Sanders points out that scholars often have difficulty distinguishing between the words of the historical Jesus and the words that the early church later attributed to him.

> Christians believed that Jesus had ascended into heaven and that they could address him in prayer. Sometimes he answered. These answers they attributed to 'the Lord'. We now want to know which Lord: Jesus before he was crucified, or the risen Lord resident in heaven? The Christians thought it was all the same Lord . . . In other terms, the Spirit that freely communicated with Paul and other Christians could be thought of as the Spirit of the risen Lord, who was in some way or other continuous with the historical Jesus.

What I found interesting, and what had never struck me in quite this way before, was the idea that the early Christians identified the Spirit that spoke to Paul and other New Testament Christians with the Jesus who walked about Palestine. If this is true, then why can we not say that the Spirit that speaks to people today is also to be identified with Jesus of Nazareth? Put more personally and specifically, maybe I can say, and maybe I should have the courage to recognize, that the voice that spoke to me when I woke up that night in bed was the voice of the Risen Jesus.

The more I thought about this, the more comfortable I became with it. And if this is so for me, why not for others too? When I hear other people talk about their religious experiences of God I find it quite natural to draw the conclusion that these are quite possibly encounters with the Risen Christ. Perhaps the two thirds of the population who claim to have had some sort of religious experience are in fact being addressed by the Risen Lord? I am not suggesting that the religious experiences of which David Hay speaks are all necessarily experiences of the Risen Lord, but we ought to be willing to assume that they *might* be. At a time when the institutional churches are in decline across Western Europe, we would be foolish not to be willing to listen to the voice of our Risen Lord even if the words are not coming from where we might expect them!

Even as I write this I can hear a cautionary voice in my head. It reminds me that sometimes people do pretty terrible things because they think that Jesus has told them to. Isn't what I'm saying here very dangerous? There is truth in what this cautionary voice is saying. There is danger here. But is there not also danger in not attending to what might plausibly be the voice of the Risen Lord addressing us? Is it not true that if we refused to touch anything that had a potential danger in it we would end up not touching anything much at all? Is it not true that if we suppress something that is in us, then there is a real danger that it will manifest itself in some other, less healthy way?

How might we begin to take our religious experiences of God more seriously? And what checks and balances can we find that will help us guard against our misreading or misusing them?

A Personal Bible

I have suggested that one way of describing the Bible is to say that it is a book that tells of how God has spoken with a people over a long period of time. The Bible tells how God spoke through a wide range of things. Let me offer you a list of some of those ways:

Nature
Special people
Ordinary people
Extraordinary events
Ordinary events
Illness
Suffering
Pain
Death
Birth
Children
Animals
Astrology
Dreams
History
Stories
Music
Shared meals
Laws
Particular places
Relationships

You could no doubt add to this list.

I believe that in addition to 'the Bible' we each have access to what I call our own 'Personal Bible' – the ways that God has 'spoken' to us through our lives. Look through the above list and then make your own. Note down the ways that God has spoken to *you* at some point in your life. Only include what lies within your experience. So if you agree that God can speak through dreams, but God has not so far spoken to you through a dream, don't put dreams on your list.

It may be that other categories come to you that are not in the Bible (for example photographs and novels) that can be added to your list. When your list is finished (it will never be really complete, but you can always add to it), next to each category note down a specific example. So if music is on your list, next to it write the name of a particular piece of music through which God had spoken to you. And next to that, if you can recall it, write what it was that you felt God was saying to you through it: see if you can find a word, phrase or short sentence that catches the meaning.

I would guess that if you put all these words, phrases and sentences on one sheet of paper, there will be a consistent message. They will give you a sense of who this God is who has been addressing you.

Now you have what I call your own Personal Bible. One of the amazing things about the Bible is that the words in it continue to speak to us centuries after they were written. They seem to stay alive. Like coals, even when they seem dead, you can breathe on them and bring them back to life. This is what the preacher tries to do every Sunday morning in the sermon: to make the Bible's words live for us anew.

Well, the same is true for the words you've written in your Personal Bible. You will find that if you revisit the experiences, they will continue to speak to you. So listen again to that piece of music; revisit in your imagination that special place; imagine yourself with that person who was so important to you.

You might like to revisit one experience in your Personal Bible each day, on a regular basis. It may well be that God is saying something different to you now from what you sensed God saying at the original time. It may be that in a time of trouble, you could name your trouble to yourself and to God, and then revisit something in your Personal Bible; you may find that God is saying something to you through it about what is on your mind.

One other thing might surprise you. Look again at your list of the ways through which God has spoken to you during your life so far. What are the three or four ways through which God has spoken to you most often? My guess is that they will be either painful and difficult times, or activities that you very much enjoy doing. Just pause and digest that latter thought. God seems to be able to speak to us often, and successfully, when we are doing something we enjoy. So we ought, as a matter of spiritual discipline, to spend time doing enjoyable things, should we not?

I have a Personal Bible, with memories of moments when God spoke to me, poems that have touched me deeply, pictures that I value, and various *bons mots* and prayers that are important to me. I read parts of it each day, after I've said my prayers and read my Bible. It's my greatest treasure.

HM

3

Religious experience in the Bible

———◆◆◆———

As well as giving us many different examples of ways that God has spoken to people over the centuries, the Bible offers a number of stories that tell how individuals received and tried to respond to being addressed by God. This chapter looks in detail at two such stories.

The Annunciation to Mary (Luke 1.26–38)

The nub of the story is the meeting of an angel with a young girl, Mary. There are several interesting things about this meeting. First, there is nothing in the story to indicate where the meeting takes place, beyond the implication that it took place inside. Nativity plays have accustomed us to seeing Mary sitting quietly on a stool. Artists often depict her reading or spinning. But the story tells us nothing about the setting. It is equally possible that she was doing the washing up, the ironing, or making the beds, or even just putting her feet up after a busy day. In short, she might well have been doing any of the household tasks that you and I have to do.

The meeting is entirely unexpected. It comes out of the blue. We know nothing of Mary's state of mind prior to the meeting, but there is nothing to lead us to suppose that Mary was expecting this to happen. And what does happen? Who is this angel?

Nativity plays have led us to assume that angels are always dressed in white, and have wings. There is nothing in the text of the story to indicate this. The Greek word that the Bible translates as 'angel' simply means 'messenger'. We are talking here about a 'messenger from God', but there is no indication as to how the

17

messenger delivers his/her message. There are presumably a number of possibilities. It may be that Mary had a vision, and 'saw' a messenger. It may be that Mary 'heard' a voice. It may be that Mary just 'knew' what the message was, and therefore from whom it came. It may even be that the messenger was another human being, through whom God spoke to Mary. All of these are possible.

As Mary receives the news from the messenger she moves through a sequence of emotions. She is, first, 'deeply troubled'; then she 'wonders' what the greeting could mean; then she doubts and asks a question; finally she accepts the message. The movement is from anxiety, to thinking, to doubting and questioning, and finally to accepting. What the story doesn't tell us, of course, is how long it took Mary to move through the sequence. We tend to assume that it all took place quickly, once and for all, and that may well be what happened. But I also find it plausible to think of this sequence taking much longer. Maybe it took Mary hours, or days, or even weeks or months after her first hearing of the message to accept it. Maybe she was stuck on the thinking or questioning for some time. Maybe, having thought and questioned, she went back to thinking again. Or perhaps she worked through the sequence over and over again, finding different levels of meaning each time. However long it took, notice that the angel doesn't leave her until it is over. She is not left to handle matters on her own.

If we think of the story as a model for this sort of experience, then the lack of time references allows all these possibilities to be available to us.

Notice the 'speeches' of both Mary and the angel. Mary says very little: a nine-word question, and a twelve-word acceptance. But the angel speaks three times, twice at some length. Perhaps all of this took place in a brief moment of time. But if the story is thought of as unfolding over some considerable period of time, then it might be that the initial message was just that Mary would have a child, and that the rest of the detail of the angel's words came to Mary as she reflected on that initial message.

The story gives Mary very little to do. It's not absolutely clear whether the issue of Mary's acceptance is a real one. The angel appears to tell Mary that she will become pregnant. There doesn't seem to be much room for discussion here. Could Mary have said 'No'? The story doesn't seem to allow for that. Where choice comes in, perhaps, is in the manner of her response to what she had been told. So maybe Mary had no choice about being pregnant, but she did have some choice about whether or not to cooperate further with the message. In this context perhaps it is significant that the only thing asked of Mary is that she should name the child 'Jesus'. By agreeing to this she indicates her acceptance of her role. We too might find it helpful to perform some simple symbolic act to signify our acceptance of our religious experience, even if it is only a quiet 'Yes'.

The story also glosses over the fearful consequences for Mary of this message. Her pregnancy will put her in considerable difficulty. What will she say to her family and friends, let alone her husband-to-be? Is anyone likely to believe this story about an angel? What is going to happen to her? Who is going to look after the child?

Another interesting aspect of the story is that Mary is offered a sign, some unlooked-for event that will authenticate her experience for her. She is told that her elderly kinswoman Elizabeth is expecting a child. I wonder if signs are less usual in religious experiences today, or whether, on the contrary, little pieces of synchronicity often occur that appear to corroborate our experience?

Elizabeth, also serves as someone Mary can talk to about what has happened to her: someone in whom she can confide, who will understand and will pass no judgement, because Elizabeth is going through a similar experience. She will be able to offer support; Mary will not feel alone through all of this.

Jesus' baptism

Then Jesus arrived at the Jordan from Galilee, and came to John to be baptized by him. John tried to dissuade him. 'Do	It was at this time that Jesus came from Nazareth in Galilee	During a general baptism of the people,

you come to me?'
he said. 'It is I who
need to be baptized
by you.'
Jesus replied, 'Let
it be so for the
present; it is right
for us to do all that
God requires.'
Then John allowed
him to come.

No sooner had
Jesus been baptized
and come up out
of the water than
the heavens were
opened and he saw
the Spirit of God
descending like a
dove to alight on
him.
And there came a
voice from heaven
saying, 'This is my
beloved Son, in
whom I take
delight.'
(Matthew 3.13–17,
REB)

and was baptized in
the Jordan by John.
As he was coming
up out of the water,
he saw the heavens
break open and the
Spirit descend on
him, like a dove.
And a voice came
from heaven: 'You
are my beloved Son;
in you I take
delight.'

(Mark 1.9–11, REB)

when Jesus too had
been baptized and
was praying, heaven
opened and the
Holy Spirit
descended on him
in bodily form like
a dove, and there
came a voice from
heaven, 'You are my
beloved Son; in you
I delight.'

(Luke 3.21–22, REB)

The story of Jesus' baptism is told in three of the four Gospels.
The accounts of Mark, Matthew and Luke (REB) are set side by
side above, in order for us to be able to see how their versions of
the story compare. A number of interesting things emerge!

Matthew prefaces his story with an account of how John the
Baptist tries to dissuade Jesus from being baptized by him, arguing that it would be more appropriate for it to be the other way

round. Seemingly Matthew and his church found it difficult to see why Jesus had needed to be baptized by someone who was 'junior' to him. This doesn't seem to have been a problem for Mark or Luke.

We are told nothing of Jesus' state of mind prior to his being baptized. What the Gospels tell us of John the Baptist might lead us to expect Jesus, and all those other people who came to see John, to be in at least a heightened state of expectation. (See the accounts of John's preaching in Matthew 3.1–12; Mark 1.1–8; and Luke 3.1–20.) But we don't actually know.

All three writers describe Jesus' religious experience happening after, and not during, his baptism, which is interesting because the act of being baptized would presumably have been in itself a semi-formal religious act. Mark says that Jesus' experience takes place as he is coming up out of the water. Matthew says that it happens after he comes out of the water, while Luke has him praying after being baptized when it happens.

It is quite fascinating to see how they vary in describing what took place next. Mark tells how Jesus saw the heavens open and the Spirit descend like a dove, and how a voice spoke to Jesus, 'You are my beloved Son.' All this sounds like a personal, interior experience for Jesus. There is nothing in Mark's story to suggest that anybody else was aware of this happening – only Jesus has the vision and the voice is addressed to Jesus alone.

Matthew and Luke tell the story a little differently. They differ from each other in how they do this, but in the same direction. They each begin to tell the story as if it was an event of which anybody present would have been aware. Luke omits to tell us that it was Jesus who had the vision: he describes it as if anyone might have seen it. Matthew alters the words that the voice speaks to: 'This is my beloved Son'. The words thus cease to be spoken to Jesus alone, but are rather addressed to all present.

The simplest explanation of all this might be that Jesus had a religious experience of which no one else knew (following Mark); that at some point he shared the experience with somebody (the disciples would be the obvious people), and with the story now 'public' it was retold and retold, gradually in the retelling becoming

21

more and more an exterior event. Anyone who has told stories will know of the tendency to make them more dramatic in the telling, in order to hold your audience; making Jesus' experience one that everybody witnessed would no doubt have made it easier for people to understand.

Although the experience Jesus had was a very powerful one, it was also quite non-specific. Seeing the Spirit of God descending on you and hearing a voice saying that you are God's Son may be enormously affirming but it doesn't tell you what to do next. No direction or explanation is offered. Jesus has to work out for himself what this experience means: he's given no clues.

All three Gospel writers make it clear that this is a turning point in Jesus' life. He does not go back home to Nazareth, where he had come from (see Mark 1.9); instead he goes into the wilderness to ponder the meaning of all this. Now the wilderness would not have been a pleasant place, but the Spirit he has just received drives him there.

Matthew and Luke go on to tell of three of the alternative ways forward that Jesus considers, is tempted by and rejects. Perhaps it is significant that they don't tell us which way forward he did accept at the time. Maybe they didn't know, or maybe Jesus didn't know himself at that point; maybe he was just clear that certain ways forward were not right without yet being clear which way *was* right. Perhaps the way forward needed to be learnt by experience, rather than being clearly indicated at the beginning. Certainly the time in the wilderness must have been very difficult for Jesus, struggling with these issues. All three writers depict the scene as not just a struggle on the human level; it also involved the devil on the one hand and angels on the other. Jesus may or may not have been aware of this, but the struggle within himself was but a mirror of the struggle between good and evil, a struggle of cosmic dimensions. And this struggle is not resolved in the wilderness. At the end of the story we are simply told that the devil departs (Matthew 4.11; Luke 4.13), the implication being that he may return. The struggle is not yet over, it will continue.

The story of Jesus' baptism may now sound much more like one of our own religious experiences. It seems to have been unexpected;

it was intensely personal and was not shared with anyone else until later; it was very affirming; but its specific meaning had to be discovered. The discovery would not be simple or easy, for it would have to take place in a setting that would be experienced as a wilderness, but it would be all right. There will be angels looking after you.

Checks and balances

I mentioned earlier the need for some checks and balances to help us avoid the real dangers of misreading or misusing our religious experiences. These two Bible stories offer some guidance.

1 In both stories we are told that an angel stays with the person addressed by God until such time as they have come to accept their experience. God does not leave us alone after speaking to us.

2 Mary is offered a sign to verify the trustworthiness of the message she has been given. She is told that her cousin Elizabeth was expecting a baby. We too might find ourselves being offered a supportive sign.

3 Mary is given someone in whom she can confide about what has happened, who will understand, accept and confirm her experience. Elizabeth's experience was not quite the same as Mary's, as it was her husband Zechariah who had been visited by an angel, but she knew what it was like to be touched by God in such an unexpected way. Mary would find in her both an ally and a friend.

It is a great help to have someone with whom you can talk about your religious experience. You won't want to share it with just anybody; it is too precious for that. But someone whose wisdom you respect can provide some checks and balances as you seek to respond to God. There is a tradition within the church of men and women who have a gift for this. The tradition speaks of them variously as spiritual directors, soul friends, spiritual accompaniers, spiritual guides. You may be lucky enough to find someone like this. But don't worry if you don't. There is a wise Eastern saying that I believe we can trust:

'When the pupil is ready the teacher will come.' Look out for someone in whom you can confide.

4 Jesus went off to be by himself for a time, to consider and reflect upon what had happened to him. You may well want to do something similar: either go away for a time alone with God to mull over your experience; or give some time each day or week to keep it in mind and ask yourself if anything else has happened that might confirm, contradict, or clarify what you experienced.

5 Jesus seems to have come first of all to some clarity as to what his experience did *not* mean, before he began to understand what it *did* mean. It may be easier to rule some things out as a first step.

6 Jesus clearly reflected upon his experience in the light of the Bible: how it might help him to understand what had happened to him, and what he was being called to do. In the story he quotes biblical passages to the devil to counter the superficial attractiveness of what the latter proposes. It will almost certainly be valuable to hold your experience against your understanding of the Bible. It may be that certain verses come to you that clarify your understanding.

7 Notice that neither Mary nor Jesus acts hastily: they both give themselves time to consider what has happened. They mull it over. This is valuable advice, for it will almost certainly take a while for the full meaning and implication of what you have received to sink in. It will take time to begin to understand it. You will need to reflect on the possible consequences of saying 'Yes' to it. It may be some time before you can give a real and committed assent to it. I am sure that God does not expect us to respond before we are able to do so.

8 When they are ready to act, both Mary and Jesus take one small step at a time. Mary goes to see Elizabeth, and Jesus goes off by himself.

There is an excellent story of a Tibetan monk who fled his country and travelled across the Himalayas to India. When he arrived he was asked how he had managed such an arduous journey, through bitter cold and snow and over such impassable mountains. His reply was, 'One small step at a time.'

What is not stated, but is clearly implied in both stories, is that both Mary and Jesus took these experiences seriously. They may have taken their time to ponder them, but they did not forget them. They thought and no doubt prayed about them, and they allowed their memory of the experience to work on inside them and to bear fruit.

Our religious experiences are unlikely to be of the intensity of these two biblical ones, but the principles of how we might reflect on them remain the same.

HM

4

God can speak to us through anything

The variety of ways in which God communicates with people in the Bible suggests that God is able to speak through almost anything. There seems to be nothing through which God cannot speak. Yet most of us go around with very fixed blinkers on, which only allow us to entertain the possibility of God speaking to us through very particular means. One of the unhealthy consequences of this attitude is that we easily end up dividing the world into good (things through which God does speak) and bad (things through which God could not possibly speak). This is not only unhealthy, it is unbiblical. The Bible offers many instances where we are encouraged to see that God has a knack of addressing us precisely through those things we are inclined to reject. Jesus gives us many examples, of which perhaps the most obvious is the story of the Good Samaritan. The man who shows the love of God, who incarnates God, in this situation, is the despised foreigner, the man least likely. But Jesus' whole attitude to those on the edges of acceptable society makes the same point: he is regularly criticized for mixing with disreputable members of society – tax collectors, prostitutes, sinners – and he replies that it is exactly among these people that he is called to go. Very often it is they who will be entering his Father's kingdom first. Jesus is amazed at the faith of certain Gentiles; he comments that their faith is much greater than that of many of the Jews to whom he was sent. So let's not decide for ourselves how or in what manner God may speak to us. God can speak through any situation, and indeed may more easily surprise us with his word through an unexpected source. I find it impossible to forget reading how Bishop John Robinson,

struggling with cancer, spoke of trying to find God in the cancer
(see James, 1987)!

Evelyn Underhill tells a wonderful story in *Practical Mysticism*:

> The old story of Eyes and No-Eyes is really the story of the mystical
> and unmystical types. 'No-Eyes' has fixed his attention on the fact
> that he is obliged to take a walk. For him the chief factor of exist-
> ence is his own movement along the road; a movement which he
> intends to accomplish as efficiently and comfortably as he can.
> He asks not to know what may be on either side of the hedges. He
> ignores the caress of the wind until it threatens to remove his hat.
> He trudges along, steadily, diligently; avoiding the muddy pools,
> but oblivious of the light which they reflect. 'Eyes' takes the walk
> too; and for him it is a perpetual revelation of beauty and wonder.
> The sunlight inebriates him, the winds delight him, the very effort
> of the journey is a joy. Magic presences throng the roadside, or cry
> salutations to him from the hidden fields. The rich world through
> which he moves lies in the foreground of his consciousness; and
> it gives up new secrets to him at every step. 'No-Eyes' when told
> of his adventures, usually refuses to believe that both have gone
> by the same road. He fancies that his companion has been floating
> about in the air, or beset by agreeable hallucinations. We shall
> never persuade him to the contrary unless we persuade him to
> look for himself.

We might usefully aim to cultivate the ability to look for ourselves,
and to notice what we see. Try to be awake to the assumption that
God might be speaking to us through the ordinary events of our
lives, and that if we keep our eyes open, we will recognize when it
happens.

Try looking back over the day and asking yourself: 'What are
the images from the day that have stuck in my mind?' They may
have been actions of others. They may have been images from
television screens or newspapers. They might have been very
fleeting. But if an image has stuck, especially if you can't quite
think why, then possibly God is trying to say something to you
through it.

If you do this regularly, you may well find that the same message seems to be repeating itself!

Some biblical models

The Bible is full of examples of what I have been describing. In the Old Testament, Amos 7.1–9 and 8.1–3 tell of four instances of God showing the prophet something. Amos is shown a swarm of locusts hatching and devouring a crop of corn; he is shown an out-of-control fire burning the land; he is shown a builder holding a plumb line against a wall to measure it; and he is shown a basket of summer fruit. Now presumably anybody might have seen these things, and no doubt some people did, but only Amos found himself addressed by God through them. Only he was able to see significance in events that many people saw.

The opening chapters of Hosea tell how the prophet took a wife at God's command, had children with her, and then found her to be unfaithful. She seems to have left him for another man. But Hosea finds that his love for her is so great that he goes and buys her back. No doubt he was something of a laughing stock! Hosea reflects that if his love for his wife is so great that he feels himself compelled to do this, how much more must God be willing to love his people who let him down? He comes to a deeper awareness of the depth of God's love through his own experience.

Jesus seems to have learnt much about God by a similar process. He wonders about the variable success of his preaching ministry and perhaps feels downcast, but then he sees a sower sowing seed. He notices that much of the seed falls in places where it will not flourish, but the sower seems unconcerned by this fact, because he presumably knows that the seed that falls on good soil will provide a sufficient crop. This must have been a common sight in Palestine, but only Jesus is recorded as drawing a conclusion about God and his ministry from it. The same is surely true about many of the images that Jesus uses in his teaching. He must have known of a man who was beaten up on the road from Jerusalem to Jericho, who subsequently found help from an unlikely source. He must have known of a prodigal son who left home and spent all that his father had given him. Jesus not only knew of these stories, but as he reflected on them he found God's teaching in them too.

The God who speaks to us through life

I wrote earlier of my conviction that life will teach us most of what we need to know, if we but pay attention to it. Here are some exercises to help open you to that wisdom of God coming to you through your own life. You will find more such exercises in the sections on a 'Rule of Life' in Chapter 8 (pages 68–71) and on creating a prayer space in Chapter 9 (pages 74–6).

1 How am I today?

Sit yourself comfortably and relax. Then give a little time to each of the following four questions.

Ask yourself: How is my body today? What is my body saying to me? Is it tired? Does it ache? Is it tense? Is it full of energy? Does it want to go to sleep? Does it need food and drink? Has it had too much food and drink? How is my body today? What is God saying to me through my body?

Ask yourself: How is my mind today? What is my mind doing now? What is it thinking about? Is it wondering what I'm going to do next? Is it preoccupied with something else, or maybe somebody else? Is it full of ideas? Is it tired and needing a rest? How is my mind today? What is God saying to me through my mind?

Ask yourself: How is my heart today? What is my heart saying to me? What is it feeling? Is it full of love? Is it full of hate or anger, or some other feeling? Is it feeling dried up and numb, unable to feel anything? Does it feel as if I have switched it off? Or does it feel full of life and energy? Full of hope and expectation? How is your heart today? What is God saying to you through your heart?

Ask yourself: How is my soul today? The part of me that longs for God and the divine. What is my soul saying to me now? Does it feel alive or dead? Am I aware of it at all? Does it long for God? Does it feel abandoned or hurt by God? Does God feel close or far away? Does it sing or does it weep? How is your soul today? What is God saying to you through your soul?

Then bring these four questions and your answers together, and ask yourself: So how am I today? What is God saying to me today through my body? What response might God be inviting me to make to what God is saying?

2 The Four Directions

I was given this prayer exercise by the Spirit some years ago, and I have used it myself ever since. I was led to understand that each of the four points of the compass, north, south, east and west, represent both a different season and a different time of the day. Together they represent Four Directions. So:

North represents the season of Winter and the Night-time. It is a place that is described by words and phrases like cold, dark, stripped bare, waiting, helplessness, hunger, emptiness, exhaustion, vulnerability, weakness, death, fear and failure.

East represents the season of Spring and the Dawn of the Day. It is a place that is described by words and phrases like new life, beginnings, renewal, hope, new shoots, inspiration, fresh energy, birth, initiatives and resurrection.

South represents the season of Summer and the Noon of the Day. It is a place that is described by words and phrases like coming into strength, power, authority, leadership, using gifts, maturity, affirmation, recognition, pleasure, relaxation, rest, Sabbath, enjoyment.

West represents the season of Autumn and the Evening of the Day. It is a place that is described by words and phrases like twilight, waning, diminishing, pruning, letting go, gathering in, harvest, burning, cleansing, discernment, judgement, reflection and commitment.

My life always seems to have something in it in each of the four directions. There is always some part of my life that is in *winter*, where it is empty and dark. There is always some part of my life that is in *spring*, where there are new beginnings, and fresh hope. There is always some part of my life that is in *summer*, where I am powerful and able to relax and enjoy life. There is always some part of my life that is in *autumn*, where there are things that need to be let go of, and others that need to be recommitted to.

On any day one of the energies usually seems stronger than the others, but if I search my life there are always some parts of it that are in each of the directions.

So, I stand upright, with my feet a little apart, and face north. I open my arms out wide, and ask the blessing of the Angel of the North on all those parts of my life that feel as if they are symbolically in the north, and I take the time to name them out loud to God one by one.

I then turn 90 degrees to face east, and perform the same ritual action, only this time I ask the blessing of the Angel of the East on all those parts of my life that are symbolically in the east. Continuing to turn to face south and then west, I repeat the action with the Angel of the South and then the Angel of the West.

My experience with this prayer exercise is that it helps me in a number of ways:

1 It helps me to stay in touch with all that is going on in my life, not just the dominant bits of the moment, and by naming them to own them to myself. So, if the dominant energy of the moment is the north, and life feels bleak and hard, then it is quite salutary to discover that there are also parts of my life in the south, where things are sunny and bright. It is all too easy to forget the directions that are not the dominant ones of the moment.
2 It helps the whole of my life to be better integrated.
3 It gives me a way of offering up the whole of my life to God.
4 It seems to make it less likely that I stay stuck in any one direction. Life is circular or, rather, spiral, not mainly linear. Things do move on, like the seasons and the daily rhythm. Using this little ritual seems to help to oil things, and keep them in movement.

I am quite clear that the intention is not to pass judgement on or try to change anything in any of the directions. You won't be able to. Just accept that things are as they are. They will change like the seasons, when they are ready, when the timing is right. And life for you, under God, will change with them.

It might be good to keep a record of what is in each of the Four Directions, as you do the prayer exercise on a regular basis, and to notice how things do move and change: even those you thought would never change; especially those you thought would never change. And to give thanks, and to pray that you may learn to trust even more.

3 Two more directions

This could be an add-on to the previous exercise, but it can stand on its own.

Stand with your feet a little apart and be aware of yourself firmly rooted to the ground. Think of yourself as being like a tree, with roots going deep into the ground. Imagine the nourishment that you draw up from your roots, which has made you who you are.

Be aware of who your roots are. Who are the people who have helped to shape you into the person you are, for better and for worse? Name them to yourself. Some of them will still be alive, some of them will not be. Some of them will be people you knew personally. Some will be people you only know about at second hand. Some will be people who wrote books or music or created things that have influenced you. These people are your roots: some you will have chosen, others you will simply have been given. Ask God's blessing on them all. Give thanks where that is appropriate; ask for healing if that is what you need.

It may be that you sense that some of the tasks you face in life are tasks that you have in some way inherited from those who make up your roots. You may or you may not choose to accept these tasks. You can decline them. You might also consider asking for the support and guidance of those who are your roots in facing them now.

But our roots go deeper. They lie in the lands from which our ancestors came, and in their cultures and civilizations. Again, be aware of them. They have helped to shape you; they are a part of your root system. Hold them before God, and honour their place in your story.

But our roots go deeper still. Read Donald Nicholl's words from his book *Holiness* and reflect on them:

One spring morning I set out at dawn and walked from the top of the Grand Canyon down the steep path that leads to the bottom where the Colorado River flows, some seven thousand feet below. As you descend the canyon you can observe on its walls layer upon layer of the sediments that have formed over millions of years, and you can relate those layers to the successive species of living creatures, both fauna and flora, that dwelt upon this earth before we appeared: Permian ferns and crinoids and armour plated fish. Observing the traces of them in this way you feel a true kinship with all those beings, knowing that both they and you trace your existence back to that first moment of transcendence when life appeared on earth. And then you start to reflect that the very eyes with which you are observing these wondrous evidences are themselves the result of millions of years of striving for light, ever since the first pin-hole eye appeared on those primitive marine creatures, the cephalopods. And you are the beneficiary of all that struggle for light, the heir to all that agony. And as you gaze at your hands or think of your ears or of your tongue it takes your breath away to envisage the innumerable strivings that had to be attempted before you could see and touch and hear and taste and speak. Had any breakdown in that series of stirrings occurred it could have destroyed the possibility for you to see and hear and sing. The breakdown was prevented by untiring faithfulness on the part of millions of beings. The mere thought of this makes you realise what an incredible hard-won privilege it is simply to be a human being; and at the same time it is an awesome responsibility. Every human being has a responsibility toward all those creatures whose agony and groaning has given him birth.

Our roots go way, way back. If we go back far enough we are connected to all the humans who have ever lived, and beyond that with all of evolving creation. Be aware of this deep connectedness, and give thanks for your place on the earth. Ask for the blessing of the angel of your roots.

Still standing with your feet a little apart rooted to the ground, be aware of the top of your head and imagine a thin thread going up from it into the heavens. Name the dreams and hopes that you have for yourself and for those whom you love. Name the dreams and hopes that you have for the groups to which you belong; those that you have for your country, for the world, for the cosmos.

Where do these dreams and visions come from? They come in part from deep within us. Some of them may be the dreams and hopes of the people who make up your root system. Some may be particularly your own. Others may come from beyond you. They may be a calling to dream that is nurtured by angels and comes from a world beyond ours to which we will travel in due time and to which we ultimately belong. They may come from God.

Open your heart, mind and soul to these dreams. We all need dreams to beckon us forward to greater and better things for ourselves and for others.

Ask God's blessing on your dreams. Invoke the angel of dreams to your aid.

HM

5

Mother Teresa's unknown story

In the autumn of 2007 a collection of the writings of Mother Teresa, *Come Be My Light: The Private Writings of the Saint of Calcutta*, was published in the UK. Many people think of Mother Teresa, who died in 1997, as *the* saint of the twentieth century. She was known throughout the world as the face of compassion and care as a result of her work among the poor, the sick, the orphaned and the dying of Calcutta, and around the world. She won the Nobel peace prize in 1979 and many saw her as the contemporary face of God. So it was surprising that while the book was reviewed in the religious press, it was not easy to find in bookshops, and very few people I came across had heard of it. Surprising, that is, until you learnt about the story that the book was telling.

It is in effect her spiritual biography; it brings together letters she wrote to her spiritual advisers over decades, and provides a moving chronicle of her spiritual journey. The story that it tells is not what you might have expected. An Albanian-born Roman Catholic nun, she first went to India to teach in 1929. On a train journey to Darjeeling from Calcutta, on 10 September 1946, made in order to enjoy a well-deserved break from her work, she had a decisive mystical encounter with Christ. 'It was in that train, I heard the call to give up all and follow Him into the slums – to serve Him in the poorest of the poor . . . I knew it was His will that I had to follow Him. There was no doubt it was going to be His work.' Christ appeared to her on a number of other occasions, calling her to 'Come carry Me into the holes of the poor. Come, be my light.' Hence the book's title.

She was impatient to get started, but there were inevitably delays as she sought the necessary permission from her religious superiors to begin her new work. She found this period of waiting very frustrating, as her letters make clear, although she later seems to remember it as a time when Christ was very close to her, and therefore as a blessed time. Eventually she was given the go-ahead on 6 January 1948, and entered her new calling. Almost immediately Christ withdrew his presence from her. 'Before the work started [1946–47] there was so much union – love – faith – trust – prayer – sacrifice. There [in Asanol] as if Our Lord just gave Himself to me – to the full. The sweetness and consolation and union of those six months passed but very soon.'

She later wrote of this time in a letter to one of her spiritual directors:

> Now Father – since 49 or 50 this terrible sense of loss – this untold darkness – this loneliness – this continual longing for God – which gives me that pain deep down in my heart. – Darkness is such that I really do not see – neither with my mind nor with my reason – The place of God in my soul is blank. – There is no God in me . . . I just long and long for God – and then it is that I feel – He does not want me – He is not there . . . Sometimes – I just hear my own heart cry out – 'My God' and nothing else comes. – The torture and pain I can't explain. – From my childhood I have had a most tender love for Jesus in the Blessed Sacrament – but this too has gone. – I feel nothing before Jesus.

On another occasion she wrote:

> I am told God loves me – and yet the reality of darkness and cold-ness and emptiness is so great that nothing touches my soul. Before the work started – there was so much union – love – faith – trust – prayer – sacrifice. – Did I make the mistake in surrendering blindly to the call of the Sacred heart? The work is not a doubt – because I am convinced that it is His not mine.

Over and over again the letters in the book describe feelings like these, and they seem to have continued for the remaining 50 years of her life, with only one brief intermission. Yet she remained to the world the smiling, compassionate face of the divine, and hardly anybody knew of her inner spiritual turmoil. If they had known, she feared that people would have thought her a hypocrite, to talk so easily about the loving God whom we meet in the poor, and yet to feel no sense of the presence of that God within herself.

The book is very powerful and deeply moving: we owe a debt of gratitude to the editor for making it available. If it were to become more widely known it could have an influence as great in its way as all of Mother Teresa's practical compassion, for it names something that is rarely admitted in public and from a source that few can question. I've talked about it wherever I get the opportunity among Christian groups and church congregations, and everywhere the response is the same. People know this experience for themselves, yet it's rarely talked about; you hardly ever hear a sermon preached on it, and people often feel a deep sense of shame and failure in admitting that they've 'been there'. Oddly enough that's rather similar to the religious experiences that Alister Hardy was interested in researching. Most people seemed to have had those experiences too, but nobody ever talks about them either! Why is there this veil of secrecy over our sense of both the absence and the presence of the divine in our lives?

Yet if you read the right books, assuming you knew where to find them, you'd soon learn that both of these sorts of experience are the commonplace of the spiritual journey. Technically they are referred to as the *via positiva* and the *via negativa*. The positive way, the way up, is when you find God in everything. The negative way, the way down, is when you are aware only of what God is not: God is a mystery beyond our understanding and feels like an absence and not a presence. In between these two sorts of experience is where most of us spend our time, too busy and too distracted to be willing and able to engage with either, and possibly running as fast as we can from both!

Yet many relationships with God combine these two experiences, the positive and the negative; often, although not always, beginning with the former and then moving on to the second, the more reflective, silence-based one, later on. Nearly all of us will go through both, very likely more than once, during our lives. A healthy church needs to embrace both spiritualities.

One of the difficulties is that because nobody talks much about the negative way, when it comes it is a great and unwelcome surprise; and because nobody else is talking about it you feel that this must be something peculiar to you, and clearly in some way your fault, because you are the only one experiencing it. Mother Teresa's letters give the lie to this.

They also make it clear that she relied heavily on her spiritual directors throughout her life. It was mainly, but not exclusively, to them that she spoke of her spiritual journey, and it was from one of them that she eventually found the wisdom and resources to begin making sense of what was happening to her. We write elsewhere in the book about spiritual direction, and I will come later in this chapter to the advice that helped Mother Teresa, but for now I simply want to reiterate the point we made earlier – that it can be enormously helpful to have somebody else to talk with about your faith journey. Yes, God does speak directly to each of us, and yes, we can for the most part trust life to teach us what else we need, but it remains true that it can be a great help to have someone to talk these things through with, someone who can act as a sounding board. That is especially true when dealing with what appears to be the absence or silence of God, not least because it is very easy to misread these situations, and self-diagnosis is rarely the best way forward. It is astonishing how even the most spiritually mature person can't see what is under their spiritual nose, although it may seem blindingly obvious to a perceptive spiritual friend!

Let me offer you a glimpse of the possibilities here. The spiritual journey, the faith exploration, call it what you will, entails both ups and downs. I take that to be a fact. You will hopefully know times of spiritual joy, when your spirit is uplifted and your soul dances. Enjoy these times, because they do not last for ever. When that joy ceases you will come down to earth with a bit of a bump: the greater the sense of joy the greater the bump, possibly! The bump isn't likely to last for ever either; in time it will probably be replaced by a sense of lightness again. Life is a cycle of these highs and lows, some higher, some lower, some shorter, some longer. This is how it is.

The lows, the bumps, might be the result of all manner of things. The fact that you are feeling down today, either don't want to or feel unable to say your prayers, and find God to be largely absent, doesn't necessarily mean that you are in the same spiritual place as that Mother Teresa wrote about. What are the alternatives?

1 The most obvious explanation might simply be that you are tired and worn out, and what you need to do is take your foot off the accelerator, slow down, have a holiday, and just be gentle with yourself for a bit. I often ask, 'What do you do for fun?' If you can't answer this question, or have difficulty in answering it, then maybe you just need a break.

   One of my favourite stories is of the priest who no longer read his Bible or said his prayers, and who felt that his faith had died on him. He was married with a working wife and several small children. 'What do you do for fun?' I asked him. 'Oh, I don't have any time for fun – there's too much to do,' he replied. 'Well, what did you do for fun before life got so busy?' I asked. He thought for a while: 'Well I used to enjoy listening to jazz.' I suggested that he stopped trying to say his prayers and read his Bible, and stopped worrying about his faith. Instead he should give himself 20 minutes every day to listen to some jazz, not as background music, but with his feet up and a glass of wine or a cup of coffee in his hand, so that he could simply listen and enjoy. We met again a month later, and he was a changed man. He had taken the time to listen to some jazz every day, and would you believe it, he'd started saying his prayers again because he wanted to, and he was also reading his Bible regularly. His faith was alive and well again. And all because he'd allowed himself some fun. It isn't usually quite as easy and dramatic as this, but you get my point. Why is it that Christians are often strangely reluctant to admit to the importance of fun, regarding it as selfish?

2 It may surprise you to hear that religious folk can get a bit over-churched sometimes. A break from churchgoing – a sabbatical from church for a couple of months, or going to another church where nobody knows you and you can just fade into the background and be there without any responsibilities – can be as transforming as 'listening to jazz each day'.

3 Sometimes your faith seems to go dead for no reason that you can see, and you wonder what is going on. Look at the rest of your life. Perhaps some other area of life is very difficult and painful at the moment: a key relationship is going through a tough time; somebody close to you has died; you're anxious about work; fearful for your health; worried about somebody you love? Sometimes if there is pain and hurt in another part of your life it will affect your relationship with God; indeed, it would be strange if it didn't. If communication feels impossible with someone significant, it may well be difficult with God too. You might expect the opposite to be true, for God to be really there for you when the going gets tough, but it often feels like the reverse. It then easily feels like you've been abandoned by God just when you needed God most. It can make all the difference to name to yourself what the real problem is and ask yourself: 'What can I do to address this problem? What small step can I make that might move it forward?'

The Gospel story where Jesus tells people not to present their gift at the altar if they are out of relationship with their brother might be addressed to precisely this situation. It won't feel as if God has accepted your gift if a key human relationship doesn't feel right, so start by putting that right first.

4 It might be that your current spiritual practice or image of God needs a shake-up and a change. Prayer can go dead because you have outgrown that way of praying and need to try something different. Rather than feeling a sense of failure, it could be that God thinks that you are ready to progress and is calling you to grow into something different. For example, I often find that someone for whom verbal prayer has dried up can find new life in being encouraged to pray any way they like but without using words. So they start praying by listening to music, or looking at pictures, or just by being silent.

5 It might be that a familiar image of God has reached its sell-by date. There is maybe nothing wrong with it as an image, but perhaps you have outgrown it; perhaps you are ready to use a different image. This again is a sign not of failure but of growth. You are ready for a deeper knowledge of God and that requires

you to find a new image. Actually, you don't have to 'find' it at all. If this is what you need then it will find you, you just have to watch out for it. You'll recognize it if you stay alert, open and watchful. But you might have to wait a while. You cannot control when or how it will come.

Remember that story of the man who fell off a high cliff. As he fell towards the ground many feet below he managed to grab hold of a branch growing out of the cliffside, and hung there. He could see no chance of climbing back up to the top, and the ground was a terrifyingly long way down. He'd never much believed in God, but felt that this might be the time to give it a try, so he shouted out, 'God, are you there?' 'Yes, I'm here,' came back the reply. 'I need your help, I'm stuck.' 'Well, let go and I'll catch you,' said God. The man looked down at the ground many feet below. 'Is there anyone else there I can talk to?' he asked.

You might just have to wait, having let go of your old image, and trust that God will provide you with another one. It might even be that the whole point of the waiting is that God is inviting you to learn to trust God more than you already do.

6 Sometimes people get confused between the *via negativa* and a time of depression. They are not the same. This is not the place for a discussion about the difference between them, but they are different. If you are feeling depressed you need to get medical or therapeutic help, not spiritual counsel. Again, a benefit of having someone to talk to is that they may be able to help you if you are not sure exactly what help you need.

The via negativa

The explanation for God not seeming to be present might be none of the above: there might be some other reason. Or it might be that God is leading you into a dark way of not knowing, and of the seeming absence of God, the *via negativa*. Remember Mother Teresa's story: she had a relatively short period of a year or so where God and Christ felt intensely close and where intimate communication seemed very easy. Then, suddenly, all that ended and she felt herself plunged into utter darkness. She continued to long for God but God no longer seemed to be there, and the absence, coming after such intense intimacy, was excruciatingly painful. It led her to question her original experience. Had she misread her sense of closeness? Was her sense of call a mistake? Deep down she seems to have known that neither interpretation was true, but her questions continued to haunt her.

As I wrote earlier, one of Mother Teresa's spiritual directors was able to offer her some wisdom that helped her find a way forward. We need to remember that what helped her isn't necessarily going to speak to us; nevertheless it is interesting to know what he said. A number of things seemed to have helped her.

First, he said that this experience was not her fault. It was not a sign of her failure. It was not a judgement from God upon her. These experiences happen to nearly everybody. They are a part of the spiritual journey. She should not take it personally.

Second, there is nothing very much that we can do about it, beyond accepting the situation. We cannot end it, or get rid of it. It is not in our power to do so. This experience will pass when the time is right and we have no control over when that might be.

Third, the fact that she cannot feel God's presence is not in itself evidence that God is not in fact present. Feelings are not everything. We also have our brain, and we should use that too and not be governed just by our feelings. Our brain tells us that God is always present even if we are not aware of it. We have to learn to trust our brain and not just our feelings.

Fourth, her thirst for God while in this darkness was itself an indication of God's hidden presence within her. It was a sign of God praying within her, and thus of God's presence.

And finally, the only response to her experience is a total surrender to God and an acceptance of the darkness. Perhaps she could come to see it as a sharing in the pain and desolation that Christ himself felt? If she could see that, then the darkness has meaning and point to it. It could be how she shares most intimately with Christ's redeeming work.

All the above sounds like good wisdom to me. It is hard to understand how a relationship can exist with no outward signs of its existence. It is not easy to understand why a God who has assured you of God's love should suddenly choose to be absent, leaving you with darkness, emptiness, absence and silence. It does not feel like a very loving way to behave.

But the tradition says that it is in fact a call to a deepening of the relationship, not a sign of its absence. It's a call to a deeper trusting in a God who is inevitably beyond our knowing. All we can do with such a mysterious God beyond our comprehension is to let go of our own hold on power, let go of any sense that we can possibly know what this God is up to, and let God be and do with us as seems best: this is deep trust indeed. It can feel pretty scary, but rationally it is possible to see that it makes sense.

While it is true that God comes to us in everything and is therefore in one sense eminently knowable, it is also true that if God is really God then we cannot begin to know a fraction of what God is; we can't begin to fathom the wisdom of God's plan; nor to grasp an understanding of God's ways. It is blasphemous to think otherwise. And somehow we have to learn to hold these two contrary, paradoxical ideas together, because they both appear to be true.

So if we find ourselves led into the darkness and the absence we need to learn to accept that that is where God wants us to be for now. That being the case, we must learn to be there, and not try to run away or fill the emptiness. We have to stay there and look the darkness in the eye; to come to trust that in the midst of the emptiness we will find what God is: a God beyond our knowing but in whom we can trust and rest, and can find in that trusting and resting something better than knowing.

There is often a stripping and a cleansing that goes on here, as we discover that God is best known when we stand naked and vulnerable before a God who feels like an absence. A God we can't find by ourselves but who comes in the seeming absence and finds us. We don't need anything in this place: nothing that will be a distraction from the real task of being here. All we need is God and our need of God. Anything else simply gets in the way.

This experience can lead to a deeper self-understanding of ourselves that is not dependent on our possessions and our status. It can lead to a greater need for silent prayer.

Some people choose this way; or perhaps better, find that this way chooses them, or that they sense that this is the way that God is calling them to be. So monks and nuns may go off into the desert. More and more people seem to be hearing a call to the solitary life even while remaining within the business of society.

Most of us will at some time sense a call to go this way. This feeling may dominate at certain seasons of our lives. Even when it doesn't, we will sometimes hear within us a summons to go for a quiet walk in the woods or by the sea, or to sit quietly somewhere and just 'be'.

Some people have this way thrust upon them. God is sought after, but is never really known. I know a wonderful old lady who has been a pillar of her church for most of her life, but she admits that she's never had anything like an experience of God's presence. She keeps going, very cheerfully, because she has decided to believe and she does, and that's that. Such people may seek security in form and order – the structures of church worship and life generally may be very important – and they may therefore be quite resistant to change.

There is, I guess, a danger of getting stuck in this dark but, after a time, comfortable and familiar place: one might be reluctant to let it go. It's not easy to embrace where God seems to have put you and yet remain open to the possibility that God might in time want to lead you elsewhere! It's not easy to find form and structure that offers meaning and shape to the darkness, and yet remain open to the sudden discarding of that structure at the in-breaking of God in everything again. And yet if we are truly learning to let go of control and allow God to do it God's way and in God's time, then that is what we have to do.

HM

6

The absent, silent God of the Bible

This absent, silent, dark God is a God who is known in the Bible. It is a God often associated with wilderness and desert. For the Bible the desert is a hot, dry, arid, lifeless, dead place, seemingly endless and where no relief is to be found. It is easy to get lost there; desperately easy, especially on your own, to face death there. It is a hungry and thirsty place. It is a place where God is not, or seemingly not.

And yet the Bible tells of God leading people into the wilderness. Israel is led there after the Exodus from Egypt; John the Baptist exercises his ministry there; Jesus is led there by the Spirit after his baptism. So it is potentially a place of God's choosing and therefore of gift.

A call to the wilderness often follows on from a personal call from God. Jesus goes there after God has called him at his baptism. The people of Israel are led there after being called out of Egypt by God. Paul goes off there after his Damascus road experience. So we should not be surprised when we find ourselves led there too.

The wilderness is often presented as a place that has to be passed through. Neither Jesus nor Paul nor the people of Israel, in the examples quoted above, stayed in the wilderness; they passed through it. As did the prodigal son in the parable Jesus told: he learnt a lot from his miserable time there; he came to his senses, left and was reunited with his father. In the wilderness between Jericho and Jerusalem, where a man was beaten up and left for dead, he found a stranger coming to his aid, saving his life, and no doubt transforming his views on foreigners for ever. His wilderness experience changed him; he was not the same afterwards.

The good shepherd goes to find the sheep lost in the wilderness and brings it safely home, rejoicing.

There are several major wilderness experiences in the Bible that can serve as models, teaching us something about the spiritual significance of the wilderness.

1 The wilderness from Egypt

The longest wilderness experience in the Bible is the story of the people of Israel's journeyings after they had been led out of Egypt by Moses. It is full of salutary wisdom about the experience!

1 It comes right after a series of powerful displays of God's providential support for the people: the miracles in Egypt against Pharaoh; the story of the Passover and the escape from Egypt; and the opening up of a safe passage through the sea. After these displays of God's power the people are invited to trust God even when there are no such special displays, even when they are absent. It's easy to trust God when all is going your way, and you seem to be getting a lot out of the relationship, but can you continue to trust when it appears you are not getting anything back? Are you just into this for what you can get, or are you into it because of a true search and love for God?

   Can you learn to love God for God's sake rather than just for your own?

2 They spent a long time there . . . 40 years is probably not meant to be taken literally, but it clearly indicates a significant period of time.

3 Many of them did not survive the experience, not even Moses lived to enter the Promised Land on the other side, and it fell to Joshua to lead the people across the River Jordan. Even if this is literally true, there is also symbolic truth in it, that the person/people who leave the wilderness will not be the same as those who entered it. It will change you. Or put it another way, something has to die in the wilderness, and something is re-born there too. There is both death and resurrection.

4 The people in the wilderness spent a lot of time complaining and grumbling: about provisions and the lack of them, about Moses and the inadequacies of his leadership, and about the providential care of God and the lack of it. They complained about lack of water (Exodus 15.24; 17.1ff.); the lack of food (Exodus 16.1ff.), the hardships they were having to put up with (Numbers 11.1ff.).

5 They suffered greatly from selective memory, which would be very amusing if it weren't so flagrantly at odds with what had been said earlier in the story about conditions in Egypt: for instance: 'Remember how in Egypt we had fish for the asking, cucumbers and watermelons, leeks and onions and garlic' (Numbers 11.5, REB); and, 'If only we had died at the LORD's hand in Egypt, where we sat by the fleshpots and had plenty of bread' (Exodus 16.3, REB).

6 They cheerfully abandoned God for a less demanding alternative, by creating for themselves a golden calf to worship while Moses is detained longer than expected up the mountain talking with God (Exodus 32). It seems incredible that they could so quickly and easily shift their loyalties and forget all their previous experience of God, but they did.

7 Yet the God who had called them out of Egypt into this desert place continued to be present for those who had the eyes to see. Food to eat (Exodus 16.13ff.) and water to drink (Exodus 17.5) was provided when they needed it; they never need go hungry or thirsty.

8 Leadership in the form of Moses was provided if they would but trust him, and that leadership was regularly supplemented with contributions from Moses' father-in-law Jethro (Exodus 18.1ff.), and a group of 70 elders (Exodus 24.1ff. and Numbers 11.16f.). They were never left without guidance; the more problematic question was whether they would heed it!

9 And God continued to show God's presence by being present in the other. The story of how God goes before them to guide the people through the wilderness is told in Exodus 13.21f. God guides them, being a pillar of cloud during daylight, and a pillar of fire by night: that is, God is the darkness by day,

and the light by night. God is always there in the other, in the opposite, in the unlikely, the contrary. Perhaps one of the reasons for being led into the dark is so that we are no longer able to see the things we are used to, but have the opportunity to see what is not visible in the light. Like stepping out at night and in the darkness being able to see the stars above us, which are invisible to us during the day.

10 Notice the little warning story of Caleb in Numbers 13 and 14. We are told that towards the end of the wilderness wanderings, God tells Moses to send some men to explore the Promised Land to which they have been led. Caleb leads such a group and returns with reports of what a wonderful and fruitful place it is, but how there are also formidable obstacles to entering it. The people are struck with anxiety; they wish that they had died in Egypt rather than be where they are now, and threaten to stone Caleb and his colleague Joshua. They are not willing to let go of the wilderness experience despite the fact that it is clearly now coming to an end. The disorientation of the new, and the need to trust God in something unfamiliar and frightening, is too much for them.

11 Notice also how not everybody in the Old Testament tells the story of the journey through the wilderness in the same way. Jeremiah and Hosea both sometimes recall the time spent in the wilderness as a sort of golden era when the people of Israel and their God walked hand in hand amid deep trust. This is unlike in the later years, after they had entered the land of Palestine and were led into all sorts of false practices as a result of living there (Jeremiah 2.1–3; 31.2f.; Hosea 2.16f.). Mother Teresa similarly looked back on her initial period of frustration as a time of rich blessing. We shall notice a similar pattern in the Gospels as they recall the story of the crucifixion in rather different ways. What was clearly on the one hand a very painful experience is remembered on the other as a time when, with hindsight, God was very close and real and important lessons were learnt.

2 The book of Job

I won't tarry long over Job; sufficient to observe that it tells the story of a man who was a passionate believer in God. God allows Satan to test Job in order to see how real his passionate faith truly is. Job loses everything, and is 'comforted' by a series of friends who tell him that this must have come about because of some failing of his; what he needs to do now is to express his deep penitence and sorrow to God and to apologize for whatever it is he has done wrong. In offering this advice the friends were probably doing no more than giving what passed for orthodox wisdom at the time. But Job will have none of it. He insists that he has done nothing wrong, he has committed no offence to God, and therefore there is nothing for him to apologize for. His friends regard this as high-handed arrogance and are not convinced. But Job prays, pleading in anguish to God, demanding that God come and state his case against him. Eventually God relents and addresses Job. He offers an awesome display of power, which silences Job; he realizes that he is in no position to question God about anything at all. Job learns an important lesson about the unknowability of God, but is vindicated because God has appeared to him.

In our context, the book of Job is a powerful statement of the importance of speaking to God about what is on our hearts, even when it may seem that it is not our place to do so. Even when the orthodox wisdom of the day says that we are wrong, we need to trust our own sense of what is right. We might indeed be quite wrong, but arguing, pleading, ranting at God clearly indicates that the relationship is alive and not dead. Just be careful not to spend so much time shouting that there is never time to listen too!

3 The crucifixion

The most powerful story of dereliction by God is, of course, found in the passion of Jesus. This is a story that the *via negativa* knows well.

Here we see that the man who strode around Palestine teaching, talking to and about God, calling disciples, touching and healing the sick, changing people's lives, suddenly falls silent. He becomes inactive from the moment he is captured in the Garden of Gethsemane. From that point on he says virtually nothing, and initiates nothing. He becomes passive and is done to by others. He is entering what we have learnt to recognize as a wilderness experience.

His disciples either actively betray him, fail to understand him, or fall asleep and go absent at the crucial moments. When it counts they deny they know him, and he is left to face the music on his own. A crowd that had appeared sympathetic and support-ive suddenly turns against him and is happy to assent to his death. He is dressed and addressed by those who consider themselves his opponents in ways that are humiliating and totally misrepresent who he is. He is condemned for something he has not done, and is led away by himself to face a slow and agonizing death, reviled by his persecutors. He is so weak that he cannot even carry his own cross to the place of execution. At the end it feels as if even the God he loved and about whom he spoke to others, has deserted him: 'My God, my God why have you forsaken me?' He dies and the world goes dark.

At least that is how St Mark tells the story. It's bleak, dark and lonely, without much sense of God's presence, and seemingly hopeless. St John tells the story rather differently, of course. In his Gospel, Jesus hands himself over to the authorities in the Garden of Gethsemane; indeed they are not able to take him without his consent. He heals the servant whom Peter attacked. He proclaims his kingship as not belonging to this world, and declines to speak to Pilate in ways that might have secured his release. He steps out carrying his own cross, and as he hangs dying he makes arrange-ments with the beloved disciple for the care of his mother in the future. He dies having said the words: 'It is accomplished.' This is a very different spin from Mark's.

It's the spin of someone reflecting some time after the event, when the horror of it has faded a little in the memory, and a deeper and more hopeful meaning is beginning to emerge. A meaning that finds some sense in what had previously looked like empty horror. A meaning more obviously from the other side of the resurrection, in the light of which it is now possible to view the crucifixion and understand it differently. To see it as the necessary and God-intended means to a deeper and more wonderful truth that could not have been imagined without it. It's the shift that Hosea and Jeremiah made with respect to the wilderness wanderings. It's a shift that if not made may leave you still in the wilderness, still at the foot of the cross, reluctant to leave a familiar place behind and to step out in trust in a God who, you have learnt, will carry you forward somewhere new.

Exercises that explore the via negativa

Below are some prayer exercises you can use that will begin to awaken you to the *via negativa* before you find yourself called fully into it, and may resource you while you are there. Some of them overlap a bit. Don't try any exercise that you don't feel ready for. You might even create some of your own.

Prayer exercise 1

Recall a time like this that you experienced some time ago, long enough ago for much of its power to be gone. Remember it in as much detail as you can.

What precipitated it, if anything?

Were you alone with this experience, or did anyone else share it too?

What did it feel like at the time? What words might describe it?

What sustained you through it? What kept you going?

Who were the angels who appeared along the way, offering support and signs of the presence of God's love?

What did it teach you about yourself and about God?

With hindsight, was there a gift within it for you?

You could sit quietly with your thoughts and feelings before God.

You could write your own book of Job: your own version of that book drawing on your own experience.

Or you might like to write a letter to God about this experience, expressing yourself as openly and honestly as you can.

Prayer exercise 2

Look back over your life, perhaps by drawing a lifeline, beginning at your birth and continuing until today, and marking on it the main events of your life.

Note where these times of absence have occurred on your lifeline.

Is there any pattern to them?

Looking back, in the context of the bigger picture of your life, can you discern any purpose or meaning to them?

Have they each been trying to teach you the same thing, or has the lesson been different each time?

If you put the lessons together, do they have a shape and coherence to them?

Prayer exercise 3

Draw another lifeline, and on this one mark the significant moments of failure in your life. Don't be hard on yourself, but be honest and realistic.

Is there any shape or pattern to your list?

What was each inviting you to learn from it?

Is there a pattern to the learning invitations?

Hold your moments of significant failure before God. Tell God about them. If it's helpful, write about them in the form of a letter. Then be still before God and notice what God has to say about them and about you, if anything.

Prayer exercise 4

There were times when the twelve disciples either didn't understand Jesus, or misunderstood him, or betrayed him, or felt his absence.

Make a list of some of those times that you remember from the Gospels. It's best not to use a Bible for this exercise. Trust your memory. Your memory is the guide you are looking for here.

Make a second list of similar moments in your own life. Again you might want to put them on a lifeline.

Put your two lists side by side. Do they speak to each other? Are there parallels or overlaps between your own list and your biblical list?

Be silent before God with your thoughts from this exercise. Don't try to excuse or justify yourself to God. Simply be yourself as someone who often fails, and be there before God.

Prayer exercise 5

Make a list of things that you once believed but no longer do. Take your time over this, and when you have finished put your list to one side.

Make a list of things that you are not certain about, about which you are a bit agnostic. Again, take your time, and when you have finished put your list to one side.

Make a final list of the things that you know you believe in, that you feel quietly confident about. Take your time.

Is this last list enough?

Supposing that it's all you have right now, what sort of faith might you be able to build on it? Where do you sense that it is calling you? What supports will you need?

Prayer exercise 6

Make a list of images of God that have been important to you during your life so far. When you've finished, put the list to one side.

Make a second list of images of God that are important to you now. Put the list to one side when you have finished.

Face God with no image at all.

Prayer exercise 7

There is an apparently universal longing for an authority parent figure. This longing can be triggered by almost any authority figure, such as a pop star, a doctor, a priest, a teacher.

Make a list of those who have been such authority figures for you during your life. You might want to plot them on a lifeline. Then name them to yourself, and put each one aside.

Let go of these authority figures, and be alone by yourself before God.

There is an authority figure who is uniquely your own inside you, given you by God at your creation. Be aware of him/her. Perhaps give the figure a name.

Ask God's blessing on this figure, and be aware of their presence with you always.

Prayer exercise 8

There are five lessons we need to learn if we are to grow as human beings. Spend a little time thinking about these lessons, about what you have learnt and what remains.

1 Life is hard and frequently unfair. You will get hurt.
2 You are going to die. You will have to let go of everything you have.
3 You are not that important. Life will continue without you.
4 You are not in control of your life. You are relatively powerless.
5 Your life is not about you. You are a fragment of something much bigger.

Prayer exercise 9

A recent exhibition in London showed photographs of patients in hospices in Germany. One picture was taken while each person was still alive, and a second picture was taken immediately after their death. The two pictures were set side by side, with a brief commentary by a writer who had spent time with them, describing the person's feelings about life and their imminent death.

Look at yourself in a mirror. Imagine what your face will look like when you have just died. Hold the two images side by side. Write your own brief commentary on your feelings about life and the prospect of your death.

Be silent before God with your thoughts.

Prayer exercise 10

St Francis of Assisi wrote of death as his sister: 'Sister Death', he called her. Take a walk with your sister death. Tell her what you would like her to hear. Listen to what she might have to say.

Imagine her with you always. There used to be a fashion for thinkers to place a human skull on their writing desk to remind them of their own mortality. Imagine one on yours. Or wonder, why might that be such a difficult thing to do?

Try living in the presence of death. There is a lot of it about, but it often remains hidden . . .

How might 'death' become a sister or a friend?

HM

7

Prayer

---◆---

People with a faith background usually think that prayer is important, but often reckon that they're not very good at it, and feel bad about that. I think that most of us are much better at prayer than we give ourselves credit for. Often the problem is that we define prayer too narrowly, because our vision of God is too small. So I suggest that we start not by thinking about what we can do to breathe new energy into our prayer life, but by looking at the bigger picture and asking: What is prayer?

Human beings have always prayed because we have a sense that there is a God beyond ourselves whom we can address; we hope that God will hear us and respond to us. The Christian gospel goes further, in saying that God is a God of love, and that this God lovingly, actively seeks us out. It is in the very nature of God to desire relationship with us. The Alister Hardy research I quoted earlier seemed to suggest that most people know of this relationship because they have some experience of God, although many of them would not use explicit Christian language to describe it.

The Christian gospel also says that because God is a loving, relating God, and because we are 'created in God's own image' we cannot be fully human without relationship with God. The Alister Hardy research appears to bear that out too, suggesting that those who have spoken about their moments of religious experience, and who therefore know something of this relationship, are more likely than other people to be psychologically well-balanced and happy.

The God we have discovered in the Bible, and in our own Personal Bibles (see pages 13 onwards), is this God who is actively seeking a relationship with us. We have also seen that the biblical God seeks to relate to us through everything. The most important things about God are that God is a God of love, and that God seeks relationship with us through everything.

I think of prayer as anything that nurtures this relationship between God and us. The initiative in prayer is not with us. God created us, and created us for relationship with God, so the initiative lies with God. Prayer is something that is primarily God's business. Our weakest longings for God and our feeblest attempts at prayer are responses we make to the initiative of God.

The God who created me for relationship with God is praying in me, sustaining and nurturing our relationship, keeping it alive, and stirring me to respond. God is always and everywhere praying in other people too.

As I go outside, God is praying in each person I meet. As we meet, the God in me meets the God in them. There is a splendid tradition, I suspect Celtic in its origins, that says when you meet someone you don't just say, 'The peace of God be with you.' Instead you say, 'The peace of God be with you both', addressing not only the other person but also the angel (a symbol of God's presence) who accompanies them wherever they go. People of other faiths make the same point when they bow to each other on meeting. God's praying thus unites me with every person God has created. God is praying in all of us.

Thus united by God's prayer, my relationship with all other human beings is transformed, for they are now my sisters and brothers. The Lord's Prayer makes this point when it begins, '*Our Father . . .*' The praying of this prayer to God unites us with all God's children, who share God's image with us. Acknowledging God as Father carries with it the implication that all other human beings are my brothers and sisters. Loving God and loving all God's children are two activities intimately bound up with each other; we can't do one without doing the other. So prayer calls me to social and pastoral action, as a practical expression of that recognized family relationship with others. When I respond I am not only responding to the needs of my brother or sister, I am responding to the God of love who calls me, and thus what I am doing is a form of prayer. Not to respond in this way is to doubt that we are family, and that God is the 'Our Father' of all of us.

Ask someone where they would choose to go in order to be open to a sense of the presence of God, and the likelihood is that they would choose somewhere out among the natural world. For most people God is most obviously present not in a religious building but in a garden or a park or out in the countryside. For all of creation is the handiwork of this God of love, and when we are in it we tend to become aware of God's love. It makes good sense then to think that God is not only always and everywhere praying in us, but is always and everywhere praying in all of creation. And if we have eyes to see this we will be able to do so. When we take ourselves out into the natural world that is what we want to do. We are deepening our relationship with God, we are praying.

As we sense the God we know praying in the whole of creation, so our attitude to creation is transformed. To fail to care for the whole created order is implicitly to fail to acknowledge God and God's prayer in it. In caring for creation we are responding to God and therefore deepening our relationship with God. We are praying.

What are the implications for you and me of this bigger picture when it comes to our attempts at prayer?

1 It is God who takes the initiative in prayer and who calls us to respond in relationship. It is God who is the primary 'pray-er'. Prayer is primarily God's business rather than ours. Sometimes it is enough just to recognize that.

   Prayer may be simply standing unprotected before God. You just wait there, open to God, and trust that God is praying in you and that that is enough. Sometimes turning up may be all you can manage, but it is enough. There do not have to be good feelings involved on your part. You may need to learn to accept that once you have decided to put yourself naked before God in prayer, that is all there is to it. You may feel nothing. You are not praying in order to feel good, you are praying because you have made the decision to give time to be consciously before God in order for your relationship to deepen so that you may grow into the human being that God has created you to become. Part of that will be your trusting that it is happening, whatever you might be feeling or thinking.

2 We have been created for prayer, because at our core is a desire for relationship with the loving God who created us, and prayer is what nurtures that relationship. And if God is truly a God of love then prayer can't, in principle, be so hard. As Sister Wendy Beckett has put it: 'The astonishing thing about prayer is our inability to accept that if we have need of it, as we do, then because of God's goodness, it cannot be something that is difficult' (*Sister Wendy on Prayer*, 2006).

3 While all human beings are created 'in God's image' and God prays in each of us, we are all gloriously different; every one of us is unique. So our ways of relating to God will also be unique to each of us. One of the dangers in prayer is the assumption that we should all pray in the same way. While we need some ways of praying together when we pray corporately, when we pray on our own we need to feel free to do so in ways that feel natural and right for each of us.

4 Prayer is primarily about our relationship with God. It is not about getting things, or changing things, or persuading God to do something God hadn't previously intended to do, although things can and do sometimes happen because of prayer. It is about deepening the relationship between God and me.

Prayer doesn't change God but it can change me. If I pray for a bike for Christmas and I don't get one, I don't stop believing in God. I learn to trust that God is saying 'No' and has good reasons that I may not understand for doing so. Or perhaps God is saying 'Not yet', and I need to learn to wait and trust. If I don't like the answer I think I'm getting then I can go back and talk some more to God about it. Prayer is about getting communication going between me and God: about deepening the relationship. We might have some stand-up rows; I might occasionally go off in a huff and refuse to speak for a bit, but I learn to keep coming back, trying to communicate, trusting that the primary task is the deepening of the relationship, and the development of trust in me. It will almost certainly lead to growth and change in me, which may not always be comfortable or what I might have chosen! And it will almost certainly lead to growth and change in my thinking about and knowledge of God.

George Appleton, in *One Man's Prayers*, wrote this wonderful prayer about a changing understanding of God, stimulated by thinking about the biblical story of Mary of Magdalene meeting the Risen Jesus in the garden on Easter morning:

> O Christ my Lord, again and again I have said with Mary
>   Magdalene,
> 'They have taken away my Lord and I do not know where they
>   have laid him.'
> I have been desolate and alone. And you have found me again,
> And I know that what has died is not you, my Lord. But only
>   my idea of you,
> The image, which I have made to preserve what I have found.
>   And to be my security.
> I shall make another image, O Lord, better than the last.
> That too must go, and all successive images, until I come to
>   the blessed vision of Yourself, O Christ my Lord.

5 Prayer is primarily about our relationship with God, but it is also about our relationships with other human beings, and with all creation. Prayer brings us into communion with the whole of God's creation. Prayer is responding in love to my brother and sister; it is responding in love and care for all of creation. Anything that does this, consciously or unconsciously, is prayer. For some people this may express itself mainly through what they 'do', their practical care of others and the environment: this is their prayer. For others it may express itself primarily in terms of 'being', a silent sense of interconnected relationship with other people and the whole of creation: this is their prayer.

6 Prayer is directing my thoughts and feelings towards God and always trying to stay open to a response: sometimes using words, sometimes not using words. An increasing vogue today

is for praying through symbols: lighting candles, putting stones in water, placing bunches of flowers in significant places at significant times. A big advantage of symbols is that when it is difficult to put one's prayer into words, using a symbol can be a very satisfying way of expressing something deeply felt. While the symbol remains in place, the prayer continues to be symbolically offered.

7 I can practise the ways of praying that others have discovered to be helpful. It's good to learn from the wisdom others have acquired over the centuries. But it can be dangerous to get too hooked on techniques, which might get between God and me and hinder our relationship.

8 Alternatively I can nurture my own natural ways into prayer, by naming to myself the activities that I enjoy and that naturally lead me into a sense of God's presence. We each have our natural way or ways into prayer. What activity do you enjoy that easily takes you into a space where you are relaxed and receptive to the divine? It might be listening to music or reading; it might be being outside in a garden or a park; it might be doing some simple physical task with your hands; it might be caring for another person, or joining in with a group activity. Whatever you enjoy doing that seems to leave you open to God, do it and see it as prayer.

It's good to recognize that God has created me able to know him through the things I enjoy. But it can be dangerous if I just enjoy myself and forget God. A way of minimizing that danger is to say a short prayer asking God's blessing on your pleasurable activity before you begin. Afterwards, take a short time to reflect on what God might have been saying to you through it.

9 It's good to pray on our own, but it is also good to pray with others; and for many people it is much easier to pray with others rather than on our own.

To summarize, it is God who initiates prayer in us and who calls us to respond. We will all have felt something of that call. It is a call to relationship. Prayer is whatever nurtures our relationship with God.

God is a loving God, so responding can't be difficult. We each have our own God-given ways of responding in prayer, which we can learn to trust.

Exploring our relationship with God through prayer will help us to grow into the person God has created us to become. It will also change our relationships with other people, and with all creation.

HM

Part 2

DEVELOPING YOUR
PRAYER LIFE

8

Creative change

Introduction

Chapters 8 to 10 look at ways to help you creatively change your prayer life.

In this chapter I look at reviewing your life with a view to changing the way you structure it. In Chapter 9 I explore ways of finding your unique way of praying, and Chapter 10 provides some resources to help you find new ways of praying and thinking about prayer.

Creative change is at the heart of the message of Jesus. This change can be in external circumstances, in lifestyle or in the way we feel, think or act in circumstances that cannot be changed. First, a few issues that nearly always arise when attempting to help people into or along the change process.

We often make 'new resolutions' but sometimes fail to keep them. We need to learn from the resolutions that *have* worked. We can be intimidated by a 'large step'; when this happens we should look for a 'small step'. Where has a small change (even a very, very small change) made a difference and how was it achieved? Congratulate yourself on the things you are able to do, and have done. This can help motivate you for future change.

Life experiences, both good and bad, can be the catalyst for the motivation to institute change, but sometimes just feeling good about yourself is sufficient. If you have been trying to change for a long time but nothing has worked, maybe it is worth trying something new as an experiment. Maybe do something you have never done before, just to see whether it works or gives you clues for what could.

Being accountable to others may often help. When we look at change it can seem a daunting task; if we involve others – friends, colleagues, spiritual directors, support groups – this can be of benefit. Groups such as Weight Watchers are good examples: members report in and are weighed each week and are encouraged by being part of a group. The details might be completely different but this principle of support and accountability might be transferred to your situation and help in changing your prayer and spiritual life in some way.

You will often find that the keys and strategies for change are already in your life; it is more a matter of identifying and using them. For example, you might say that you have a problem with discipline in your life so can't pray, but regularly go to the gym. It is worth considering whether the problem is not self-discipline but motivation. What other ways are there to pray that are more in tune with your interest, personality, circumstances? How could you transfer the discipline of going to the gym to structuring a prayer life? The changes need to be realistic and you really need to believe that you can achieve them so that you structure success into your prayer life. We believe that is what God wants.

Reviewing your life

A review of your current life can be the start of the change process. This could be tied in with a holiday, a retreat, a day's walk or just a short 'time out', which gives you an opportunity to:

STOP and look at your life.
LOOK at what you see and ponder on it.
LISTEN to what this might say to you.

A way to start is just to note down facts about your life, without trying to make any sense of them to see what has happened over a period of time. You could do this chronologically, and divide this up into various aspects such as work, social, leisure, learning, family, relationship with God. Or you could do this in a linear fashion, putting down dates and columns; or in a non-linear fashion by writing headings randomly on a page and seeing how they might join together. Another approach might be to draw a picture or use photographs – or any other method that helps you gain an overall view of your life. You can also do this by just thinking about the facts of your life, but writing them down can help you to step back when the point comes to reflect and perhaps identify any patterns and clues to the future.

Although this can be a quick exercise to begin with, there is value in returning to it a number of times, to let your memory work and give time for things to 'bubble to the surface'. Allow time for your unconscious to work on the material you have produced and see what it might be saying to you. Some questions you might ask yourself are:

What is prominent?
Does anything surprise you?
Does it look like a pattern or is it chaotic?
Does it encourage or discourage?
Where are the things that have been easy?
Where are the things that have been difficult?
What has touched me?
What has made me feel alive?
Are there links to be made?
Are there problems that could be springboards?
Are there gifts I have not noticed before?
Are there transferable skills to be used?
Are there painful things that still hurt?
Are there things that bring joy?
Are there challenges that I have forgotten about?
What has changed in my life during a given period?
Are there new things that could be followed up?
What positive or negative feelings are evoked and what can I learn
    from them?

In the end this is a spiritual exercise, although it can be useful not to try too hard to make something 'spiritual' if it is not. You are just looking for 'clues' as to what might be there for you. It could take a while to become aware of anything; you need to stay with it and have faith that there is something there that God wants to communicate.

Thinking in a more focused way about God can also be useful. Being aware that God has been in charge of your life over a given period, you might then ask yourself:

What sort of God have you experienced?
A God who has cared for you and made everything easy?
A God who has been giving you a hard time?
A God who wants to shake you up?
A God who wants you to rest and be still?

Or:

What sort of God has been in charge of your life these past months (weeks, days)?
What words might describe this God?
What name might be appropriate for this God?
What might this God's name be for you?

Suppose that the God who has been directing your life is a good and loving God, and that what has happened has in fact contained a gift (however unlikely that may seem!). If you assume just for the moment there has been such a gift, then what might this gift have been? Do you want it? What might God be hoping that you will do with this gift? What might nurture it?

Perhaps you could end this type of self-questioning by saying a simple prayer to God expressing the thoughts and feelings that have been evoked in you.

Changing the structure of your life

Your review might result in a desire to change the way you structure your life, in big ways or small ways. Certain Christian traditions find putting this structure into words helpful, and using such a 'Rule of Life' might help you.

A 'Rule of Life' can sound quite intimidating, and the type of thing that only monks and nuns follow. In fact, we all produce something similar when we attempt to plan our life to achieve our goals. Here we are looking at goals related to your prayer and spiritual life but they all, of course, interconnect with other goals. An example of this type of structure is St Benedict's Rule which is concerned with spiritual growth in an atmosphere of prayer and work within a monastic setting. The structure of Benedictine monasteries attempts to order people's lives to achieve these things by periods of work, prayer, worship, study and silence.

In contrast, the lay Third Order of Franciscans asks each person to produce their own rule (based on a common framework, see <http://orders.anglican.org/tssf/About/The_Rule.html>), which is reviewed annually. A lay order is for people engaged in everyday life, and so this could be helpful to you.

The Third Order Rule of Life consists of a list of areas which each person is asked to consider and then make specific in their own life. These areas might be appropriate for you, or the list could be modified for your particular tradition and put into your own words. It might then form the basis of a review and commitment towards a spiritually healthier and more sustainable way of life. The following is an example of how one person modified this Rule of Life framework.

God's presence – to find opportunities to experience God's presence.

Review – to review my life in the light of my calling to follow God.

Lifestyle – to practise temperance in all things and have regular times of study, reading, service, fasting and rest.

Retreat – to arrange to have regular times of contemplation and meditation.

Thinking – to study, think, and discuss God's Word and its applications to the world.

Work – to engage in honest, open-hearted work compatible with my faith.

Simplicity – to use my possessions as a trustee and to care for God's world.

Obedience – to obey God's Word and be accountable to other
Christians.

Community – to participate wholeheartedly in the church
community.

Witness – to live and speak in a way that gives witness to my
faith.

Giving – to set aside resources to serve God and others, and to
practise hospitality.

Worship – to seek opportunities to worship and praise God.

Prayer – to seek opportunities to pray.

It may be that some of these categories are difficult or inappropri-
ate in your particular circumstances, but others might be helpful
and challenging. For example, in today's society obedience might
be particularly challenging and require considerable thought as to
what areas of authority (written, institutions, people) you could
submit yourself to.

The methods described above might help you to think, review,
evaluate and structure your life to bring God and prayer more into
focus. You could also sketch out a diagram like Figure 1 to help
you see whether you think that your life is in balance in the way
you want it to be.

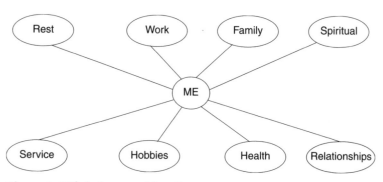

Figure 1 Life balance spider diagram

Add other categories if necessary or change the ones suggested
until you feel it represents your life. Then perhaps evaluate the
balance in terms of the time or energy you spend on the various

aspects and consider whether you need to make changes. You could use smaller and larger 'balloons' to represent the amount of time and/or energy spent on each area and compare that with another set representing how important each area is to you. Comparing the two might be an eye-opener!

A more contemporary and focused example of a review is found in Susan Jeffers' book *Feel the Fear and Do It Anyway*. She encourages us to think in a similar diagrammatic way about all the areas of our life and focus on the way the spiritual influences them. Susan Jeffers says of this process: 'If we do not consciously and consistently focus on the spiritual part of ourselves, we will never experience the kind of joy, satisfaction and connections we are all seeking.'

In considering the balance of life it is worth thinking about the biblical concept of 'rest' and the way this was incorporated into Jewish life by the Sabbath and its rituals. Where is the place of rest in your life?

Henry (pages 204–5) describes the way he incorporated this into his life by taking a three-month sabbatical from his work. You might like to skip to that passage and read his experience.

Finding your faith community

When we are thinking about making life changes it is important to consider the communities to which we naturally belong. These can give us support and a place to relate to others and share our lives. They can both help and/or hinder us in the change process.

We are all part of groups such as families, clubs, institutions and many others, but most of us also need a place where we can go for challenge, support, encouragement, and growth of our faith. Such a place has been described as a 'faith community' to distinguish it from all the other valuable communities to which we belong. Where is yours and will it, and the people in it, help or hinder change?

The early disciples gathered together, as described in the Acts of the Apostles, as a natural part of their new-found faith to hear the apostles teaching, to have fellowship, to break bread together

(Communion or Eucharist) and to pray (Acts 2.42). A community of faith is, at its best, unlike many other groups in that it has shared values that cut across race, class, professions and age, with group members being linked by faith in Christ.

Church and its ancillary groups are types of faith communities but are also social institutions made up of fallible human beings. The gatherings together can be uplifting and give us fresh energy and courage to go back into life and follow Christ in our chosen way. But the reverse can also be true, and this can apply in any denomination or tradition. Church can be a place of restriction and boredom providing social control. It can eat up our life in endless committees and small-time politics. I often meet people who need to leave church for their personal faith to survive as well as people who say, 'I don't know what I would do without my church'. The important thing is knowing for yourself what church is for you at the moment!

The Spirited Exchanges network was founded a number of years ago in New Zealand and is now in the United Kingdom. It helps people who can't find a church that works for them and/or find they must leave to survive. A common experience is that people still feel the need for a community of faith and they seek creative ways to achieve this. Some people find like-minded friends, others start groups that might just meet for a meal and discussion. For others it could be an internet interest group that keeps them going or perhaps meeting with a spiritual director. We all seem to need some human contact to help us along the way.

For the vast majority Christianity is both individual and corporate in its expressions. This inevitably creates tension in attempting to be yourself and yet belong and many need to find creative solutions for this. For example, one person I know was encouraged to stay in her church when she admitted to herself that going there was mainly about meeting her friends; she needed to find different ways of expressing the other spiritual aspects of her life.

Our experience is that relationships with others of faith are important and it is worth seeking radical and creative solutions to meet that need. If you are in this situation of struggling to find a faith community that works for you, then consider the following.

- Give yourself a break from church to see how it feels. Maybe identify the bits you miss and the bits you don't – this might help you choose a more appropriate community.
- Try other churches and groups to see what they feel like – sometimes in doing this you can find that with all its problems you like your own tradition best and decide to stay.
- Get in touch with Spirited Exchanges UK to seek out others who may also be struggling (visit <www.spiritedexchanges. org.uk>).
- Maybe leave church for a while and find friends individually or in groups that you can discuss your faith and pray with – many return to church from choice after a while.
- Find a spiritual director or good friend(s) who will help you in your walk with God.
- Just try something different that is none of the above.

RG

9

Exploring prayer and you

———◆•◆•◆———

Take as much time as you need to find the prayer that is appropriate to your essence.

Give yourself time to make a prayer that will become the prayer of your soul. Listen to the voices of longing in your soul. Listen to your hungers. Give attention to the unexpected that lives around the rim of your life. (John O'Donohue, *Eternal Echoes*)

Introduction

We believe that there is a unique way for you to pray and it is not so much about 'knowing' a lot more but discovering this way for yourself. It is a matter of finding your own voice. This chapter attempts to help in this by giving suggestions on finding yourself space, and thinking about how and when to pray in the day.

Finding a space

Finding a space to pray includes both the place itself and, if you create your own space, deciding what to put in it.

There are likely to be places that are already prayer spaces for you. You will have places where God has been real for you at some time in your life: places where it is subsequently easier to feel close to God. Try to name some of them. It might be in a church, art gallery or beautiful building. It might be a place in your own home. A window with a view. A favourite chair. Even your bed!

Many find it is outside. Perhaps a corner of your garden if you have one: or a place in a park, or open space. It might be a place with a view, a seat, a tree, a pond. Or just a place where you walk the dog! Any place where God feels close.

It's very possible that these are places you naturally feel drawn to, without any conscious prayerful intent. Is it possible to spend time in this place regularly? Perhaps daily, or once a week, or once a month? You could establish a pattern of being there and of trying to be open to God when you are there.

You might go with a particular intention in mind, or you might not. You might find it helpful to begin by asking God's blessing on your time there, and end by wondering to yourself what God might have been saying to you during the time. Often there won't seem to have been a 'message' and the benefits of your being there will be felt only gradually over time.

Alternatively you might want deliberately to create a place for prayer. If you could create a prayer space in your home or garden, where would you choose to make it? Often just asking yourself that question and thinking about it for a minute or two is enough for you to be able to recognize where that space is.

Few of us are lucky enough to have a room we can set aside, but there might be a corner somewhere. You can pray sitting, kneeling, or standing – or any way you want. Some people use a prayer stool, or some cushions. Hands up, hands together, down by your side, whatever helps.

A number of factors will influence your choice.

First, will you use your prayer space alone, or with others? If you share your home with other people, then you might need somewhere where you can be apart.

Second, when will you be using your prayer place? At set times? Or just when you want to? The advantage of a set time can be that it helps you to get into a rhythm of prayer: you know that at a certain time this is what you will do. If so, then choose a time that will be easy to keep. Many people find a rhythm of this sort very helpful, but also recognize that they may often be distracted from it. So make it as easy for yourself as possible. Choose a time that suits you best, rather than a time when you think you ought to be praying! And decide on how long you'll spend there. Again, set the bar low. It's better to commit yourself to ten minutes and find that you can do that and want to make it longer, rather than commit to half an hour and ending feeling that you've failed.

Third, what do you want to do in your prayer space? To sit quietly, to read, to say a Daily Office, to sing, to listen to music, to look at something, or simply to talk to God? The aids you use will depend on where your prayer space is. In a public space you can either use the aids that are there – probably natural things – or items you can carry in your pocket, like a rosary or a small cross. In your own home then you can use anything you like:

an icon or religious picture
a lighted candle
incense or joss sticks
natural objects, like stones or flowers, perhaps made into an
    arrangement
music
books
a Bible
any other objects that are of special importance to you, such as an
    old photo, a postcard, or a significant quotation.

Again, don't feel that you *have* to have certain things there. Choose what feels right. You can always change them; indeed, over a period of time you probably will. You might make the arrangement of your space fit the church's calendar for instance, or the year's seasons, or your changing mood.

All this may make it seem that creating a prayer space is rather complicated! That's because we have tried to cover a whole range of possibilities. To begin with it's probably best to keep it simple, with one idea, and then allow it to evolve. Remember that the aim is not to create a prayer space packed with all sorts of prayer aids that will be the envy of others! It is to create a space where you can be before God, with things near to hand that will help you to pray better.

Finding your way

Finding your own way of praying needs perseverance and confidence. It sometimes means going against the accepted wisdom and practice of your particular tradition.

There is an unspoken tendency in all Christian traditions to make some prayers and activities a 'litmus test' of spirituality. Particular models or practices seem to dominate the thinking and become the 'norm' for almost everyone.

This tendency seems to occur across the whole spectrum of spirituality, from 'speaking in tongues' to 'centring prayer' and all things in between. Many of us have sat in groups thinking, 'This is not working, but is it just me out of step?' If you were to talk to others in the group you might find that some were feeling the same as you, but thinking that it must be *their* lack of spirituality or faith!

These thoughts can be taken into and can affect our own prayer life; you continue using methods that are the norm for your group even though they do not work for you. They are all just methods and as with any method, can become an 'idol'. There are, of course, times to persevere and stick at things as they may just have gone stale. However, there are times to say, 'This is not working for me and has never worked. What else is there?'

You need to have the courage and confidence to know when something is not for you and it is time to try other things. For example, introverts in charismatic traditions and extroverts in contemplative traditions can have a really tough time in finding their own way to pray. It may not be that they need to change their tradition or denomination, because other aspects of it may suit them; they may just need to break out from its norms. If that is you, why not try some new things!

Finding a rhythm for your day

A Jewish rabbi once said: 'Dawn and dusk are basic times to pray, because then you have day-time and night-time consciousness at the same time' (Rodger Kamenetz, *The Jew in the Lotus*).

An important part of considering prayer in our life is to find out *when* to pray. Monastic Christian traditions usually incorporate a rhythm of prayer into their day, with appropriate liturgy for each part of the day. Many of us will not have the same control over our lives but there may be things we can do that make a difference.

Our modern culture tends to cut us off from the natural rhythm of our bodies and of the day. We think we have to be on the go 24/7. With artificial light available all the time, we never have to stop. We can eat whenever we want. With mobile phones and email we are never out of contact. There are seemingly no limits. But it does not have to be like that: the day does naturally offer us a shape, although we will each respond to it a bit differently.

Part of being ourselves is to learn about our natural daily rhythm, and begin to trust and accept it, to see it as a part of God's gift to each one of us. Simple things like knowing when we are likely to concentrate best on prayer. Ask yourself whether you are a morning, evening or midday person, and then find ways of making use of that information. You could also consider how each part of the day has something different to say to you.

The night

Night is a time of natural darkness, and we may be reluctant to face it because of ancient fears we have of darkness. Perhaps the challenge is to learn to trust the darkness as a symbol of mystery and the unknown. The reality often is that what feels like impenetrable darkness is actually nothing of the sort, and when our eyes adjust to the dark we realize that we can see more than we thought. Indeed we find that we can see things we couldn't see in the light, like the stars!

Once we fall asleep we enter a dream-like world where our usual control on our thoughts and feelings has less influence. All manner of insights and anxieties surface and work themselves out, leading often to a sense of recreation and refreshment in the morning.

You may find that if something is really troubling you then you will wake in the night worrying about it (perhaps like wrestling Jacob in Genesis 32.22–32). In the middle of the night the issue can seem insoluble.

One way of dealing with this might be just to realize that you are not thinking straight at that hour and try to go back to sleep. Or you might be more helped by getting up, making a cup of tea, sitting down, lighting a candle and *being* with whatever is troubling you, until you can hand it over to God before going back to bed. Often in the morning it is less of a problem!

Waking

> After the absolution of the night, the dawn is a new beginning.
> (John O'Donohue, *Eternal Echoes*)

The rising sun can be a symbol of the giftedness of life and the new day: we don't produce it, it is given. The women went to the tomb of Jesus at the break of day and found unexpected new life there. So the beginning of the day is a good time to be still and waiting for whatever will come, and maybe for saying a morning prayer over a cup of tea.

Morning

The morning has often been seen as the time when work is planned and begun. It is a time for us to engage with the world. God created us in his own image, which among other things surely means that we were made to be creative. Creativity begins here, however humble and ordinary the task. Each morning is a new beginning and a fresh start. The Holy Spirit came upon the first disciples at Pentecost in the morning, and they were filled with new life to do unimaginable things and be unimaginable people. The new life flows into us as gift and flows through us into the lives of others as a blessing, without our having to do anything except let it happen. So a brief prayer to ask God's blessing on your work might be the most appropriate – maybe on the way to work.

Noon

Noon marks the end of the morning and offers a pause before the afternoon. It's a time to stop and reflect: to collectively renew our energy with shared food and drink, after the morning's work.

It might be a time to go deeper. Jesus was crucified at noon. The sun is at its strongest at noon. It is also a time of quiet: birds and the animal kingdom are silent at the hottest part of the day. It is as if the world needs a pause from doing and a time to just be. Many cultures encourage a siesta after lunch but even a brief rest as part of a lunch break might be helpful.

Late afternoon

As we move towards the end of the working day we are faced with the realization that our work is never truly completed. There is always more to do, and another day to do it. Moreover, all the work that we do complete will pass away and disappear. Nothing lasts for ever, or at least nothing that we can do.

In the story of Jesus' passion the late afternoon is the time of his entombment, when his body is laid to rest. He had to wait and trust upon God's activity to renew it with life.

For many this is the period of transition from our place of work back to our home and family. Our best energies may be spent, we may face a stressful journey home, and all too often we bring to our nearest and dearest the very worst of us. It can be a difficult transition: a threshold moment for the balance in our life between our work and the rest of our life. Some need space and time to find themselves, others need conversation and company. How we manage to cross this threshold speaks volumes about the state of our being.

Evening

The evening is a time to lay down the roles and masks that we have worn through the day, and to find and be ourselves. For some it is a time to party, for others it is a time to relax with the television, a film, or simply over a meal with friends. The Last Supper (Luke 22.7–23) and the shared meal at Emmaus (Luke 24.13–35) both happened in the evening.

It is a natural time to review the events of the day, both our own and the world's. As the light fades it is maybe inevitable that our thoughts will be drawn to our own mortality, and we will find ourselves reflecting on the great questions of life. Why am I here? What am I for? What is the point of it all? And as we prepare for bed we prepare also to let go of another day of life. We forget that some will not wake in the morning. We know not where we go during the hours of darkness. We have to let go into the dark and to learn to trust things that we do not know and have little control over.

HM and RG

10

Finding new ways to pray

————•◆•————

Introduction

This chapter is inspired by a collection of Prayer Cards which were displayed in Soul Space at Greenbelt over a number of years. They are a collection of things to try in prayer, ways of thinking about prayer and how God works in our lives. Included here is a selection, written by different people, of some of the most popular ones, and others that give some idea of the variety of creative ways that people find helpful in approaching prayer. As always, this is just a starting point; you can modify them in any way to suit you, your personality and your tradition. In addition I hope it might inspire you to seek for yourself new and creative ways to pray.

Remember that if a certain method does not work for you, sometimes it is worth persevering, sometimes coming back at another time, or sometimes letting it go as being not for you. You may have to look beyond these.

A fuller collection of the Prayer Cards can be found at the Annunciation Trust website (<www.annunciationtrust.org.uk/Prayer%20Resources>). More suggestions about ways to pray can be found in Henry Morgan's book *Approaches to Prayer* or on the website at <www.annunciationtrust.org.uk/approaches/>.

RG

Blogging as prayer

On one level blogging is a way of conveying information: items of news, links to other websites. On another level it's a scrapbook, a means of collecting interesting quotes, pictures, sound and video files. Or it may be an easy way to keep in touch with a scattered family, distant friends: sharing mundane details that only resonate with people who have a close connection.

Blogging is all these things to me. But the daily discipline of adding an entry to my website also serves a deeper spiritual purpose. I would explain this in three ways.

First, blogging *is a daily discipline*. It is a means by which, at the end of every day, I permit myself time to sit down and reflect back on the time just passed. The events of the day, conversations, things seen, heard, read: at the computer, before my fingers strike the keyboard, all these are given a second thought and – not every time, but quite often – at that point new thoughts emerge, discernment comes, ideas and inspirations arise.

I may not end up posting on the blog my deepest, most poignant or personal thoughts, for reasons of confidentiality (where these involve others) or decency (in the words of Gerard Manley Hopkins, like everyone else's my 'mind has mountains, cliffs of fall, frightful, sheer, no-man-fathomed' which are best avoided in public). I may instead end up posting a link to an interesting article I've read.

But the process is the important thing, and that's my second point: that *adding an entry* is a way of celebrating that new things have happened that day. New insights, new encounters have demonstrated the richness in even the most ordinary of times and places. Posting something different each day is a challenge in recognizing these things, of sharing the joys that are there to be discovered in my mundane, everyday life.

The third spiritual aspect of blogging is that I do this on *my website*. There may be millions of other bloggers on the world wide web, but no one writes like I do, no one else's website looks like mine. And so this is an extension of me.

Blogs and bloggers, of course, get criticized for being self-obsessed or exhibitionist, and putting yourself 'out there' online does carry the potential for such pitfalls. But I've always been a writer, always best expressed myself through the written word, and so the blog seems an ideal vehicle for me to communicate in a way I enjoy and which is in some ways most 'me'. I find it a deeply satisfying way to end each day: playing with words, clicking the keys, communicating with friends and strangers some joys, some insights freshly appreciated. The friends and strangers are important to me, but if they weren't there reading my blog I'd still find the writing fulfilling.

So, is blogging a way of praying? I recoil a little from such a naked suggestion. But if praying is a way of engaging in a spiritual quest, involving listening and creatively attempting to express what is heard and understood, then blogging can be that. It is, for me, some days.

John Davies (www.johndavies.org)

Colourful prayer

What colour do you associate with anger?

If you asked that question to a room full of people you would get a variety of different answers. Colour is of very real importance to each of us, but the significance of a colour is likely to be different for different people.

From our early experiences, now long forgotten, we are often left with colour associations; different colours came to be associated with various feelings and emotions. For example, someone may associate anger with the colour black, another with the colour purple, another with orange.

Try the following exercise. Remember a time when you were very angry. What is the first colour that comes to mind? Repeat this with a variety of different scenarios, such as a time when you were very excited about something, very pleased, anxious, happy, and so on. In this way you can build up your own colour code to match your feelings.

Sometimes it is too difficult and painful for us to express our feelings in words. At such a time it might be that we are able to express them in colour and shape. Colour can become for us a means of reaching out to others and to God.

To colour your prayer:

Spend a few moments becoming still and centred.
Identify an issue that is very much on your heart and mind and
about which you would like to express your feelings to God.

Be focused on that issue. See what colour or colours come to mind.

Use these colours to make your prayer in whatever shape that comes.

Praying with colour is not an attempt to create a work of art or a picture; it is a way of deepening our relationship with God.

Sister Gabriel

Daily Office

For some people using regular set prayers each day can be a help in finding a prayer space. For others it will be too constraining but it might work for a while and then they need to find something new.

In some Christian traditions Bible-reading notes are used and can be helpful. There are many 'Throughout the Year' books that give daily readings and prayers. As with everything, these daily reading books can become a burden and there is a need to treat them more as just tools to help you to pray rather than as ends in themselves.

The Church of England offers the Book of Common Prayer and *Common Worship: Services and Prayers for the Church of England*. These include prayers for morning, evening and night. These can be used on your own. People can get great encouragement knowing that these are being used at the same time all over the world.

The internet offers other versions of the Daily Office from all sorts of traditions. Just Google 'Daily Office', see what you get and try some. The Sacred Space website at <www.sacredspace.ie> is an example of a site offering some spiritual help each day.

You may also like to consider compiling your own Daily Office, collecting together inspiring passages and prayers that are helpful to you. Angela Tilby has published hers in *The Little Office Book* (1998) and you could use this as an example.

You might also use other things that inspire you, like pictures and music; you could make these a regular part of your day.

Perhaps just beginning collecting for a Daily Office might give you some fresh inspiration for creating a prayer space in your life.

RG

Distractions in prayer

Conventional wisdom tells us that when we seek to be silent and open to God – no words or thoughts, just being present to God in the silence and emptiness – then inevitably distractions will come into our minds: wandering thoughts and feelings that take us away from what we are trying to be.

Conventional wisdom also says that when this happens we need to notice that it is happening and then gently bring ourselves back to our intention to be present to God in the silence and emptiness. Perhaps having a word that we repeat, or an image that will bring our attention back, can aid this process.

Much of our prayer time is likely to be taken up with these distractions, and it can feel frustrating to be seemingly spending so little time actually praying. Conventional wisdom says that we need to stick at it. It may well get better with time and practice. Even if it doesn't, the very business of trying is itself praying.

I have no doubt that there is deep wisdom in this conventional advice, and that we will do well to heed it. However, I also sense that there may sometimes be another way of looking at it. I wonder if we might be better served by taking these distractions a bit more seriously. These thoughts and feelings that clamour for our attention when we try to be silent and still may have something important to say to us. They might be telling us what is preoccupying us. They could be giving us valuable information about the movements of our own spirit and even of God's spirit within us. Perhaps they are an important part of who we are; do we perhaps need to be willing to bring them into God's presence, rather than constantly trying to gently dismiss them?

If we go with them perhaps they will spin themselves out and we will know that they are not that important.

Perhaps we could talk to God or Jesus about them? 'As soon as I try to be present before you, Lord, I find that my mind keeps going back to . . . and I don't know why.' Perhaps taking them seriously and allowing them their space before God will allow us to understand them and realize what they are trying to tell us. Maybe God will be able to say something to us about them.

Or maybe, could we try to enter into dialogue with them? 'Oh, it's you here again! Why do you keep coming into my thoughts and feelings just when I'm trying to do something else?' Try listening to what they might be saying to you. It may be that they are friendly, and not something of which to be fearful.

Equally, of course, they could be thoughts and feelings within us that we are afraid to face, or reluctant to bring before God, but which God is inviting us to explore during our prayer time together. A persistent distraction often points to a barrier that has grown up between ourselves and God or perhaps between ourselves and others.

So, sometimes, our distractions in prayer are actually invitations to explore something deeply with God, and not obstacles to our relationship with God.

HM

Drawing and using a labyrinth

The primitive labyrinth design, with its twisting and tortuous path, was adopted in medieval times to symbolize the pilgrimage to the Holy Land, or the way to salvation through the cycles of life, death and resurrection.

Recent years have seen a revival in the art of making garden labyrinths and mazes (the former being distinguished by having only one path). An indoor one can also be made, at far less expense and trouble. The process is a contemplative activity in its own right; a dedicated act of attention and true prayer.

The labyrinth depicted here (Figure 2, on p. 88) embraces the two main characteristics of medieval Christian designs: an equal-armed cross and rotational symmetry.

You could construct your own labyrinth using a soft board, pins and strong cotton. Work on the labyrinth for a set time in silence then have a period of meditation.

Figure 2 A labyrinth

The site <www.lessons4living.com/drawing.htm> shows how to draw a finger labyrinth, which you can use as a means of meditation. Use your finger to trace around the labyrinth, while thinking about the process and what it might be telling you about your journey and the twists and turns to the centre. It might give you insights into your place in relation to God and prayer. Using a labyrinth might become important in your prayer life on a regular basis, or something that you do occasionally.

If you want to be more ambitious <www.lessons4living.com/build.htm> describes how to construct a full-size labyrinth, which can be marked out with stones, rope, or other materials you have to hand.

An online labyrinth simulating the one set up in St Paul's Cathedral in the year 2000 can be found at <http://rejesus.co.uk/spirituality/labyrinth>. This takes about 45 minutes to complete.

RG

God basket

Find yourself a basket or box and put this somewhere in your prayer space. Write on the box:

I am God. Today I will be handling all of your problems. Please remember that I do not need your help. If life happens to deliver a situation to you that you cannot handle, do not attempt to resolve it. Kindly put it in the 'something for God to do' basket. It will be addressed in *my* time, not yours. Once the matter is placed into the basket, do not hold on to it . . .

When you pray and come to those things you are finding it difficult to let go of, try writing them down and putting the prayer or concern in the God basket. The idea is that this will now help you leave the concern with God, so try not to look at it again.

It may help you to fold the paper so that you don't read it again. Then destroy it in some way. A symbolic way might be to take it outside and burn it, letting the smoke disappear into the air.

HM

Holding cross

A holding cross is a small wooden cross, about 4 inches long and 3 inches wide, with the arms set not quite horizontal, so that the fingers of one hand can wrap easily around it.

Having a holding cross in your prayer space could be a useful resource for a prayer time. Just holding it without saying any words can remind you of God's presence. It is also small enough to be carried around; knowing that you have it with you or being able to hold it briefly can be a source of strength. It could be a way of creating a 'mini-prayer space' wherever you are. The holding cross can be a great resource for people who are ill or depressed or grieving. Just to hold it can bring great spiritual comfort.

RG and HM

The Jesus Prayer

The standard form of the prayer is:

Lord Jesus Christ, Son of the living God, have mercy on me a sinner.

There are, however, many minor variations in the wording. Basically this is an adaptation of the prayer of the blind man outside Jericho (Luke 18.38), and it is similar to the prayer of the publican (Luke 18.13).

Its origins are probably in the desert spirituality of the monks of fourth-century Egypt, where emphasis was laid upon inner mourning and upon the need for God's mercy. They also recommended the repeated use of a short phrase as a method for maintaining the continual remembrance of God, and so moving into a kind of prayer without images or words. Thus, despite being a prayer in words, the Jesus Prayer may lead into silence.

Its use became more widespread in the fourteenth century when it is particularly associated with the monks of Mount Athos in Greece. Some of these monks developed a physical technique in which the head is bowed, the eyes (if open) are fixed on the place of the heart; and the rhythm of the breathing is slowed down and coordinated with the words of the prayer.

At the same time the person praying seeks 'to descend with the intellect into the heart'. By the heart is meant the moral and spiritual centre of a person, the place where a person becomes most truly personal, and at the same time closest to God.

This level of prayer has been attained by many Christians using one word or a phrase, over and over again. St Francis would spend whole nights in prayer, just repeating the words 'My God and my All'. Other saints have had their own favourite words. (It is perfectly possible to use the Jesus Prayer with a rosary, substituting it for the Hail Mary.)

In the Orthodox tradition, the prayer is used primarily as a way into imageless, contemplative prayer, while in the West it is more commonly used as a prayer of the feelings and emotions, being linked with devotion to the humanity of Jesus.

HM

Journalling

My journal is a trap in which I can catch and hold on to otherwise fleeting thoughts, feelings, insights, experiences, dreams and fantasies. Many of them have no meaning for anyone except myself.

However, others have had very practical implications. It has been an invaluable aid in my research and my writing.

(Lawrence Osborn, *Paper Pilgrimage*)

You'll need a notebook that is durable and flexible, suitable for writing/drawing/sticking in. Or you could use a cassette recorder or a laptop. It's good to:

- date entries
- keep it private
- be honest: no self-delusion/no castigation/no escapism.

And 'write fast, write everything, include everything, write from your feelings, write from your body, accept whatever comes' (Tristine Rainer, *The New Diary*). It is written 'to enable me to ask definitely by forcing myself to put yearnings into words' (*The Journals of Jim Elliot*).

Consider these questions:

- Who is it addressed to? God? Myself?
- Will it cover all areas of my life: spiritual/secular/dream/family/ professional?
- If so, should I have different sections for each area? Or is it OK to let them be muddled together?
- What techniques might I find helpful?
- Might it be helpful to write as unsent letters?
- Or as dialogues, with anyone I like?
- Or as daydreams?
- Or should I use diagrams and pictures?

Using code letters may be helpful:

A	action
I	idea
P	unresolved problem that will require more thinking
PR	prayer
M	meditations, and reflections on biblical or other texts
V	voices, of my unconscious
D	dreams
F	fantasies
R	review

But remember, there are no rules.

Journalling has value for reviewing and looking for trends and developments. It will probably be helpful to reread what you have written from time to time, maybe once a week or once a month, in order to spot any themes. Does the same question keep recurring? Have you clearly moved on with some issue?

You can use your journal to enrich your prayer life.

You could divide a page into two columns, recording prayer in one and answers to prayer in the other. This might also be helpful regarding discernment on a decision you have to make. Try writing the pros in one column and the cons in the other, and keep revisiting your list until it becomes clear what you have to do.

Your journal can be a place of self-examination.

It might be helpful to write prayers, even letters to God – be honest!

Writing rather than saying can sometimes aid concentration.

Noting moments of joy and anger may lead to deeper worship.

Books that began life as journals include Dag Hammarskjöld, *Markings*; Annie Dillard, *Pilgrim at Tinker Creek*; C. S. Lewis, *A Grief Observed*; Henri Nouwen, *The Genesee Diary*; *The Diary of Anne Frank*.

HM

Lectio Divina

This very ancient model of Bible study has four parts:

Lectio (reading)

Read the passage through slowly and carefully and study what it says.

Meditatio (meditating)

Reflect upon the ideas and insights of the passage. Personalize the message either by hearing the words as spoken directly to you, or by imagining yourself into the event.

Oratio (praying)

Dialogue with God about what you have read and learnt. Respond personally to anything God has said to you through the passage. This deepens our relationship with God. A heart-felt reaction of some kind may occur. Any of four kinds of prayer may be appropriate here:

adoration and praise
confession
thanksgiving
intercession.

Contemplatio (contemplating)

Sit quietly, be still and listen, open to God.

HM

Prayer with my body

For many years I have practised *lectio divina* as described in the previous Prayer Card. It is a very old way of meditatively reading the Bible, but you can also do that with your body.

With *lectio divina* of the body you can listen to the story of every part of your body.

Silence

Sit comfortably. Breathe slowly. Gently focus your attention on your breath without trying to control the rate of breathing. Note the way the air feels as it enters your nostrils, flows down your throat and into your lungs.

Give yourself time to become accustomed to this rhythm. Then let yourself become aware of the wave of oxygen as it enters, coursing through your limbs down to your toes and out to your fingers.

Lectio (reading)

Having become aware of your breathing, now let your awareness go to the various organs and parts of your body: brain, lungs, heart, stomach, liver, intestine, kidneys, bladder, genitals, eyes, ears, nose, lips, teeth, skin, and so on.

As you breathe, give thanks to God for each of these organs, and for any part of your body that you choose. With the breathing, focus your awareness on each organ, noticing and allowing yourself to be mindful of its ongoing work within the larger whole. Take as much time as you need to attend to each organ. Notice if there is a particular area of the body that calls for your attention or that has a special significance, or that brings memories forth.

Meditatio (meditating)

Choose one organ from those you have attended. Focus kindly your awareness on that particular part of your body, adding this prayer: 'I will thank you because I am marvellously made' (Psalm 139.13, *Exciting Holiness*).

As your attention remains with one particular organ, notice if you have any feelings, fears, misgivings, anxieties, questions, or thanksgivings. What memories come to you? Concerns? Associations? Allow yourself time to pay attention to any images or colours that come to mind. Perhaps a line from a song or a poem will come to you during this time of focusing.

Oratio (praying)

Gather your thoughts and feelings into a prayer. Give thanks for your body, for any particular organ and its ceaseless working. Become mindful of those in the healing professions who help people who have an illness that affects this particular organ. Pray for those who are ill and for those who care for them.

Finally, allow yourself to become aware of the deep connections of the human family, for we are very much alike in the structure and arrangement of our physical selves. Let this connection enter your awareness; pray for the whole human family.

Contemplatio (contemplating)

After your prayer, let yourself receive the silence once again. Imagine your body encompassed by a gentle, illumining light. Rest in this illumined silence.

Gideon van Dam

Living with mystery

I have a friend who speaks of knowledge as an island in a sea of mystery. It is a lovely image – let this, then, be the ground of my faith.

All that we know, now and forever, all scientific knowledge that we have of this world, or ever will have, is as an island in the sea.

(Chet Raymo, *Honey from Stone: A Naturalist's Search for God*)

This quotation hit me like a blow to the head when I first read it, and has stayed with me ever since. What I know, what humankind will ever know, is but a small island amid a vast sea of unknowing and mystery. The edges of the island will shift as new things are learnt and old things are forgotten, but the mystery remains huge and overwhelming and touches us everywhere, wherever we look.

This is so true on so many different levels. I have just made myself a cup of tea, not in itself a very challenging task. But if my making of a cup of tea was totally down to me I would be in deep trouble. I don't know how to grow tea, let alone harvest it and prepare it for the tea-bag. I might be able to milk a cow but I don't *know* how to do so. I don't know how to grow sugar and harvest it either. I would be hard pressed to make a cup to drink it out of or a spoon to stir it with, let alone a pot in which to boil the water.

So just such a simple task, which I undertake several times a day without thinking about it, potentially reminds me first of all of how dependent on the skills and knowledge of other people I am; and of other people from all around the world. My cuppa is, as they say, 'the product of more than one country'.

On another level, I know relatively little about myself and the people I love most. The woman I see most of actually spends the majority of her time not in my presence! I have not known her for most of her life. I generally do not know what is going on in her body, let alone what is going on in her mind or heart or soul. I have some clues about those things but I can't actually *know* very much, and I'm kidding myself if I think otherwise.

This is just as true of myself. There is a part of me that I know quite well. I have lived with him all my life but I am constantly learning new things about him. There is a vast amount I don't know and never will. I don't know where I came from before my birth, and I don't know when or where or how I will die, or what will then happen next, if anything. I am in many ways a mystery to myself.

If I think about the world I live in, well, I don't *know* very much about that either. When I look up to the heavens, I know I'm looking into infinity and that it is a very long way away: further than anyone can measure or even imagine. If I look at a small plant through a magnifying glass or microscope then I see detail beyond my wonderings. And I don't *know* any of it.

I don't even *know* very much about God. God by definition is beyond our knowing: a vast, dark, silent emptiness. We may sense God's presence from time to time. We may believe that Jesus has shown us something of his nature, sufficient of God's nature even. We may feel confident that in one sense we do know God. But, in another sense, however true that may be, God will always remain beyond our knowing. God is too great and beyond us, for us ever to *know* God.

If we suppose that this small island of knowing that we have amid its sea of mystery is intended and indeed good, then what is its purpose? Why is it like this? What might it be trying to teach me about itself, and about me?

It might increase my sense of interdependence, not only with all other human beings but with all of creation of which I am but a small part. Even if only humans are aware of it, everything in creation seems to share in this mystery. We might go so far as to say that mystery unites us.

So, maybe we could usefully learn to approach all of life with a sense of mystery, wonder and reverence.

It might usefully teach us a little humility.

It might deepen our need of prayer and of worship, and it might change what we hope for from prayer and worship.

HM

Nature walk

Begin with a recollection of God's love for you and his presence with you.

Take a deep breath of fresh air and reflect on the wonder of this all-pervasive gift that keeps you alive; of the unseeing providence of God who holds you in existence and is continually creating you.

As you begin to walk, allow your senses to come alive. Look around you, notice the colour, shape, movement, beauty of what you see: a tree, flower, the sky, clouds, a face . . . Delight in it all, enjoy it, rejoice . . . Reflect on the gift of sight and thank and praise God . . . aloud if you can.

Listen to the variety of sounds, even the tiniest ones . . . voices, wind, animals, water . . . even to the seeming silence. Be glad for the music of sound, delight in all you hear. Reflect on what your sense of hearing means to you . . . and express your gratitude to God the giver of this gift.

Feel wind, sun, the air . . . a stone, a leaf, the bark of a tree, the ground under your feet, the clothes you wear . . . reflect on your use of touch in expressing affection, in physical work, in playing musical instruments, writing . . .

Imagine your life without this sense of touch. Express your gratitude and praise. Smell the scents around you . . . the atmosphere, fresh grass, flowers, plants . . . Delight, rejoice, express your gratitude.

Taste an edible berry, a nut . . . and at your next meal become aware of the subtle tastes of various foods, savour what you eat and drink, delighting in it.

How grateful do you feel for your senses? What has been evoked by this exercise? Express your gratitude naturally to God, aloud if possible.

Now, or later, move on to reflect on your life and let gratitude arise for all that you genuinely appreciate in your life. Express your feelings spontaneously in whatever way seems right to you.

Sister Gabriel

Prayer walking

Put on some shoes and step outside. The place on which you will walk is holy ground.

You can prayer walk anywhere if you believe that God is everywhere and interested in all people and all places. If you walk in places where there is hurt or pain or the memory of bad events, then your prayers can be intercessions. Anywhere you walk your prayers can be of thanksgiving for the places and people you see en route. Or you might simply enjoy listening to God as you go where your feet take you.

Prayer walking can consist of stops at a series of predetermined 'stations'. Perhaps the bus station and the fire station would be on your route, where you would pray for those who work there, who use these places and their services. Other less literal stations might be to stop outside a school to pray for the pupils, their families and those who teach; a row of shops to pray for those who work there and whose lives involve frequent journeys to and from them; an industrial site, a leisure park; a bridge over a motorway to pray for those on faster journeys.

Prayer walking can involve symbolic actions – writing prayers for the sick on ribbons and tying them to the railings of the health centre; putting prayers for sailors into small pieces of wood and dropping them into water that will carry them out to sea; petitioning for peace by slowly circling a military establishment or offering a stranger a daffodil.

Prayer walks might be enhanced by an openness to unexpected meetings or events. Someone may stop you outside their house to ask what you are doing; the ensuing conversation might result in your praying with them for their family and neighbours. A security guard might misunderstand your intentions entirely and ask you to move off the factory premises, and if the spirit of this exchange is good then the conflict might be energizing for all involved.

If you are planning a prayer walk you might elect to choose a particular theme. A walk I once led connected four well-known gateways or entrances in the city centre, and at each one we stopped to consider the comings and goings of the people who use them, the politics and spirituality of inclusion and welcome, and pivotal points in our own lives.

In one town that had been recently flooded we followed the waterways, stopping at various points to pray for the people who lived on and nearby them, our prayers involving cupping water and skimming stones as well as silence and spoken words. Once, as a way of praying, I spent a day walking in a large out-of-town shopping centre; during the afternoon I sat in a coffee house composing prayers for the shoppers and the centre workers based on what I had seen and heard.

Any place carries the potential for prayer. Prayer walking relies on the intentions and perspective of the person walking in relation to the environment they are in. If you sense that no place is out of bounds for God, and you can carry that sense with you every time you step outside, then in theory *any* everyday walk can be a prayer walk.

John Davies

Praying with the Bible

First, select a passage. Read it through slowly, concentrating on each word, and with the intention of reaching an understanding of the passage as a whole. Then try one of the methods below. Perhaps try more than one. It is important to remember that what is helpful for one person may not help another, and that what helps you now may not help you next week!

1 Read the passage again until a word or phrase 'hits' you. Pause and reflect on it; allow your mind to follow whatever attracts it. When your reflection runs out of steam, go back to the passage and continue reading, until another word or phrase 'strikes' you. When you get to the end of the passage, go back and read it through again, in the same way. Keep rereading until you have had enough.

2 See if you can identify a phrase in the passage that seems to speak to you. Don't worry about what it is or what it means. It may well be that the phrase chooses you, rather than you the phrase! Repeat the phrase over and over again, slowly, perhaps in time with your breathing or heartbeat.

3 Read the passage through as if it had been especially written just for your benefit. Allow it to speak to you.

4 Try to visualize the scene described in the passage. You might even try drawing it. It doesn't matter if you are not an artist! No one is going to see what you draw. Draw 'stick people' if you like. Allow your imagination to fill in the gaps in the picture. What might be there but is not mentioned in the text? Try involving as many of your senses as you can:

How does it look?
What sounds can you hear?
What smells are you aware of?
Is there a taste in the air?
Can you reach out and touch anything in the scene?

What happened the minute before the scene you have visualized? And what might happen immediately afterwards?

5 Imagine that you are there. Who might you be, on the edge of the story, watching what happens? Do you have a role in the story? Watch the scene unfold. Do you get involved? How do you feel? When the scene comes to an end, what do you do next? Suppose you write a letter or an email soon afterwards to a friend, how do you describe what you witnessed and the impression it left on you?

6 Imagine yourself as one of the main characters in the story, perhaps the main character. Hear the words and actions addressed to that character as addressed to you. How do you respond? How do you feel? What will you now do?

7 If you enjoy a bit of biblical criticism why not have an imaginary conversation with the writer of this passage. What does he/she mean? Would he/she write the passage in exactly the same way today? If it is a synoptic passage, put the various synoptic parallels together and imagine a conversation between Mark, Matthew and Luke, discussing the merits of their different accounts. If you are really enjoying this, introduce some other characters into the conversation!

8 What great truths does the story teach you? How might you apply them in your own life?

9 Are there other stories that have echoes of this one? Other stories that have some of the same characters or places? Can you shed more light on this story by comparing it with other stories?

HM

Praying through the body

My body moves to the cupboard where I used to store the muesli before I moved it.

Or takes the turning to work when going to the seaside.

Or wakes much earlier than it need while on holiday, and I had been anticipating a good sleep and lie-in.

Habits are embodied and my mind has to engage to remind it of changes. And that typifies a general view I had of the body as something needing to be instructed and, perhaps in one reading of St Paul, controlled.

But I've discovered that my body remembers things that my mind cannot recall and knows things that my mind can never have done. Like the time that I needed a leather needle to complete a project. In frustration at not having one on a Sunday, I went out to clear the garage, only to find when sweeping up exactly the needle I required. Even now I have no idea how it came to be there.

Or the times when my body has stood up from whatever I have been doing at a desk and headed off, much to my mind's bemusement. Once it wanted to walk two miles into the centre of York from the university and I couldn't understand why. I said to myself as I left, 'I might as well take a book to read, since I've no idea what I'm doing.' I had a good walk and sat down on a wall opposite the Minster. I'd never done so before and the different view was interesting. After a minute I thought that as I wasn't doing anything, I would read my book. I had just opened it when my brother walked up to me. He was on a mystery coach tour from a music week some 50 miles away – I had no idea he was on the week, let alone any means of knowing that he was coming to York. And he

101

certainly had no idea until they arrived ten minutes previously. Ah, that's why I'm here on this wall, I thought. And we went with his friends and had a great day.

There is a bit of me that would like to say such events are rare in my life in order to appear normal. They happen reasonably often. And sometimes with a strong disagreeing dialogue – I can describe it no other way – between the body and the mind. I've discovered that there have been occasions when the mind has overridden the body when the latter was right. And probably many more times that I do not know about.

But if my body knows such things that the mind does not, perhaps it knows God in a way that my mind cannot. And I've started exploring the way to ask the body questions in prayer, moving from the argument of not understanding what it is up to through to acceptance and appreciation. 'What does my body say about this?' I might ask. And I'm surprised to discover not only that it answers, but has insights that can transform the mind's emotions and my subsequent action.

Part of the struggle was the theology I'd received. Surely the body is there as the 'natural man' to be subdued and controlled from its impulses? Of course, the body has desires and can certainly sin when I do not choose to place its action in the way of following Christ. But in that it is no different from the mind. The split, I've learnt, is not a body/mind one, the latter renewed and the former subdued, but one of a complete person, one in a natural state moving to a spiritual one, body and mind.

'I'm thirsty,' my body said very clearly. Having seen P driving his car, I had followed him to his home. Formerly a stalwart member of our worship band, he had not been to church for many months and did not return calls. As we parked a fellow church member in the car with me asked what I was going to say. 'No idea,' I said; my body replied, 'I'm thirsty.' As we met at the front door, I said to P, 'I'm thirsty. Any chance of a cup of tea?' And he let us in and we had one. The church leaders asked me about what I had said, what I had prayed. My mind agreed with their looks of derision. But that man never missed another service for all the years I was there. Only much later did he tell me the whole story and thank me for accepting him as a friend without comment; it had enabled him to return. He didn't know it, but he was thanking my body, not my mind, which, like the leaders, had nagged out all those 'ought-to's' at me.

I cannot pretend that it is easy. I'm on a learning journey of exploration. This PhD brain often won't accept the body's wisdom or that it has a right to speak, seeking to explain it away or in an about-face then trying to claim it as projection. Although where else does the Holy Spirit dwell, if not in the body, I wonder? What else is it that makes people's faces shine, their lips smile, hearts be glad – all unconsciously? It is in the confidence of the Christian credo that I continue, for it is the body that will be resurrected, not an unembodied mind.

My body continues to be astonishing in the way that God uses it to speak to me. The body may take me somewhere surprising or, and I can use no other word for it, speak to me: 'Go into York', 'Turn right', 'I'm thirsty'. But it is sitting in prayer explicitly asking and being attentive that some of the best has come. It can be equally surprising and transforming. I'm learning a new way of praying.

David Pullinger

Praying with stones

Stones can be used to help you to pray in a variety of ways. Here are some suggestions to get you started.

- Pick a stone – just an ordinary stone, but each is part of God's creation. Each one is unique, like us, created and loved by God. Really look at it, its colour, its shape – dip it in water and see how the colour changes. What messages does your stone have for you; what is the 'water' that shows you in your true colours?
- Hold your stone and notice its temperature change. Maybe this is how you feel when you pray and are 'held' by God, or perhaps you would like to feel held but do not?
- Look at your stone – is there anything in the colour/pattern/ blemishes that helps you get in touch with something in your own life, in your own spiritual journey?

- Does your stone have crystals that sparkle in the right light? What makes you 'sparkle' and what is the 'light' that helps you to sparkle?
- You might like to make a pattern with some stones – perhaps each stone will have a particular meaning for you (maybe each stone represents a person you want to pray for, or an event in your life). As you lay the stones down pray for the person or event each represents.
- You could carry a stone in your pocket or bag, and when you touch it remember to pray. Pray for whatever is on your mind at that time – and remember to thank God for his love.
- Is there something you want to ask God to forgive you for? Hold the stone and pray about this thing, ask God to forgive you and allow the stone to drop gently into the water. Feel the weight of your sin washed away.
- Thank God for the insights you have received from holding your stone.

Jane Russell

Sacred space

Finding a sacred space for ourselves can be important and it can be useful to ask the question, 'Where do I go when I want to find God?' Three illustrations might start you thinking.

Susanna Wesley, a busy mother with no privacy, would sit in a rocking chair with an apron over her head, praying while John and Charles and the rest of her large family talked and played around her.

Mahatma Gandhi loved to sit in front of his spinning wheel, which reminded him of the life of struggle for the poor.

Precious Ramotswe in *The No. 1 Ladies' Detective Agency* by Alexander McCall Smith found her space to mull and ponder under a nearby acacia tree.

We asked a number of people, 'Where is your sacred place?' And these are some of the replies:

in the bath
a walk in the country
a walk on the seashore
by the sea or river
in an empty Cathedral
in my room
going fishing
in an art gallery
sailing
on the train
in the car
in the gym
just sitting quietly
hanging out the washing.

Some of these might give you clues where yours might be. So:
Where do you find *your* sacred space?

RG and Liz Lang

Silence and the senses

Often it is good simply to be silent and still before God: to try to empty the mind as best we can, and just to wait upon God. But this is not easy! Unless you are very experienced in the life of prayer, and have a spiritual guide to accompany you, you will almost certainly need to take something with you into the silence. It may be a biblical word or phrase, a symbol or a picture. Or it may be that you can use your senses.

Centring prayer

Centring prayer is a method of contemplative prayer in the Christian tradition, although people of all faith paths use this form. As Gregory the Great expressed it in the sixth century, 'its focus is resting in God, being in communion with the Divine in an attitude of silence'. It has some similarities to Eastern meditation in that it involves the use of a single word, repeated like a mantra:

possibilities for this include Jesus, peace, shalom, love, Abba. Like a mantra, the repetition of the word serves as a focal point, a marker to return to when distracted by other thoughts.

Centring prayer begins with the intention to be with God. Some practitioners advocate doing it twice a day, in sessions of about 20 minutes each.

The format is simple: choose your sacred word, or phrase, position yourself comfortably, and slowly repeat the word or phrase silently or out loud. When thoughts intrude and your mind starts to wander then come back to repeating your word or phrase. Let your words be something that you keep coming back to. Conclude the session gradually and gently.

Although you might feel that you have received insights or new understanding around the sacred word chosen, that is not the point of centring prayer. In fact, practitioners are encouraged simply to return to the word rather than follow the train of thought.

Thought is seen as an impediment to the experience of God that is the reward of contemplative prayer. As the author of *The Cloud of Unknowing* wrote: 'If you strive to fix your love on him forgetting all else, which is the work of contemplation I have urged you to begin, I am confident that God in his goodness will bring you to a deep experience of himself.'

You can use the principles of centring prayer but have something other than a word or phrase as the thing upon which you focus:

Sight

Focus your attention on a simple object, like a lit candle (or it could be a painting or a photograph). Don't think about it. Just look at it. Allow yourself to concentrate just on the candle. When your concentration wavers, as it surely will, just bring it back to the candle again.

Remember that the aim of the exercise is actually not looking at the candle at all, but rather looking 'through' the candle to the emptiness beyond where God is. You are using the candle as a way of clearing your mind, creating a space where God can enter.

Sounds

You can do much the same thing using sounds. This time focus your attention on your hearing. You might just be aware of what you can hear. Name the sounds that are loud and close by and then gradually name those that are further away until you are concentrating on those sounds at the very edge of audibility.

You might choose to play a CD of natural sounds: water running, the sea, or wind through the trees.

For many people an easy way into silence is through listening to music. Musicians might achieve a similar sort of thing by playing their musical instruments and focusing on the sounds they produce.

Again, you are using your hearing to hear 'through' the sounds to the silence around and beyond them, where God is. You are using your hearing as a way of clearing your mind, creating a space where God can enter.

Smell

You can also use your sense of smell. You could burn joss sticks or incense. You could light an 'aromarizer' with natural oils in it. You could simply be aware of the scent of flowers in the room.

Breathing

Another way in is to focus on your breathing. Not to breathe more deeply or shallowly than usual but just to breathe normally, and then to concentrate on your breathing. Be aware of your body taking air into the lungs, and then expelling it. Concentrate on it, and allow your concentration to clear your mind of other things. If your concentration wavers, just bring it back to your breathing again.

You might find it helpful to imagine yourself breathing in the life-giving Spirit of God, and breathing out sin and pain.

The whole body

You might try being aware of the whole of your body. Sit with your back straight, your hands relaxed and open on your thighs, and the soles of your feet flat on the ground. Imagine that there is a thin piece of string attached to the back of your head, running taut up to the ceiling so that your body is held upright.

Now, start by being aware of all the sensations in your feet. Don't move the feet, just be aware of all the sensations that are there. Take about ten seconds. Then move up your body to your ankles, and notice all the sensations there. Next your knees, then your thighs, and so on, right through to the top of your head.

When you have been all around your body once, do it again, slowly and gently. You may notice all sorts of odd aches and pains that you didn't realize were there. You may feel that your body is trying to tell you something! But just let them go and move on. Many people find this a very effective way of clearing the mind and thus preparing themselves for prayer and God.

HM

Synchronicity

Synchronicity can be defined as 'a meaningful coincidence of two or more events, where something other than the probability of chance is involved' (Jung).

It is synchronicity when another person does something that meets a need of yours, about which they knew nothing; or when a need of yours is met by outside circumstances; or when you have a dream, vision or premonition about something that then happens.

I have the quite frequent experience of just the book I need 'jumping off the shelf' at me in a bookshop. Or of picking up a book to read at home and finding to my surprise that it speaks to something I am concerned about, although that was not consciously why I picked it up.

A friend of mine, a very practical, feet-on-the-ground sort of person, told me how he and his wife were looking to move house but couldn't find what they wanted, no matter where they looked. One day, coming home from his job in London, he accidentally got on the wrong train and had to walk home by a different route.

His journey took him straight past the house they had been look-ing for and had been unable to find. They bought it and have lived there very happily ever since.

Some time ago I was wandering through the National Gallery in London, as I often do, and was struck by a picture of the crown-ing of the Virgin that I must have seen before but had never really noticed. Later in the same visit I found myself very taken by an image of the Virgin and Child. I spent some time examining and thinking about both images. A month or so later I found myself reading a book by Jung where he talks quite a lot about the feminine, especially Mary, and Dante's *Divine Comedy*, which also features the feminine heavily. Then I had a powerful dream about a feminine figure who spoke to me. Now it seemed to me difficult to deny that something was going on here! My attention was being drawn to something. Jean Shinoda Bolen says (in *The Tao of Psychology*) that 'in the experience of a synchronistic event, instead of feeling ourselves to be separated and isolated in a vast world we feel the connection to others and the universe at a deep and meaningful level'.

My experience is that there is frequently something 'accidental' about these things; there seems to have been an element of chance about them; they were not altogether what you had planned.

Most of us, I think, have this sort of experience more often than we realize. Reflect on some of the most significant moments in your life.

- How did you meet the most significant 'other' in your life?
- How did you come to be living in your present home?
- How did you come to get the job you presently do?
- What have been the moments of important growth in your life?

We may intuitively recognize these moments: something feels right that is not easy to define but of which we have little doubt. Oddly, the timing often seems to have been right, and we might well have not been so receptive a short time before.

It seems as if there is a strong undercurrent in life and that we, for the most part, splash about on the surface. Sometimes the undercurrent comes to the surface and we experience it; sometimes we sink and then the undercurrent bears us up. I wonder if this is what generations of Christians have called grace?

My experience is that these moments of synchronicity often seem to happen in clusters. There are times when a lot of such moments occur and others when it seems as if nothing is happening at all. The 'cluster' moments are usually times of change in my life. So it pays to watch out for them, and to learn to trust them when they occur. They frequently lead to good wisdom, although sometimes they do not *appear* to lead anywhere. They may help us to trust life and the providential care of God more deeply

HM

Using Active Imagination

One night I had a very vivid dream, which disturbed me. I felt that it was somehow significant as it remained with me, but I didn't know how to interpret it.

Was it coincidence that at the time I was reading a book called *Inner Work* by Robert Johnson, subtitled 'Using Dreams and Active Imagination for Personal Growth', and in it he described how this could be done. I was intrigued and not knowing what to expect decided to give it a go.

The first step, I was told, was to be in a place where I would be alone and undisturbed. I then took a notebook and pen, lit a candle and prayed that whatever emerged would be of God. Then I emptied my mind except for my remembrance of the dream and the people in it: myself, a frog and a kingfisher. To my amazement the three of us started a dialogue that led us to go on a journey. This started by entering a cave, but we have since been through forests, up and down hills, by rivers and many other places, and as we travelled we encountered different characters, some of them animals, each one identifying themselves and joining us on the journey, soon becoming integrated with the others. The frog, who is the wisest character although the most insignificant, interprets what is going on: each character is a part of myself. There are now ten of us! I have identified hitherto unrecognized grief (in the form of a chained gorilla), and rage (in the form of a bear), good and bad characters (the latter I was not at all keen to welcome at first). As we journey together we are becoming more accepting of each other and are gradually being transformed. At times, when we are struggling and seem to be lost, we become aware of God's presence in the form of a dazzling light which overwhelms us. Then it gradually fades and we are as we were before, though aware that something momentous has happened. We are overawed for a while before we continue on our journey, knowing that God's presence is still with us.

I have no control over what I write. It streams from my unconscious and I can hardly keep up with the dialogue, which is at times hilarious as the characters squabble with each other but also help each other, and often what comes out is very profound. The sessions seem to last about an hour and it becomes clear when it is time to rest. The journey is ongoing and I do not know where or when it will end.

I have found it helpful and indeed important to be able to share what is going on in my imagination with someone I can trust. I have a spiritual guide who fortunately knows about using Active Imagination; she has encouraged and affirmed me in this process and validated it so that I don't feel I am 'off the wall'.

It has been and continues to be an amazing experience. I have always had a vivid imagination and I do believe that God is using this to help me to an understanding and acceptance of myself, the good and the bad, and his acceptance and valuing of each of these parts of me, transforming me and integrating them into, one day I hope, a whole person, the one he created me to be. Trust is one of the important characters in the story, and it is in this spirit that I continue my journey.

Mary Hillard

Using the rosary

A rosary is a string of beads for counting prayers in a pattern of prayer and meditation. Various aids for counting prayers seem to have been used in Western Christendom from as early as the fourth century. This particular form begins to appear from about the tenth century.

A popular way of using it is to start with the crucifix, on which the Creed is said; the next five beads are used for the Lord's Prayer (1), three Hail Marys (2, 3, 4), and the Gloria (5).

Where the pendant joins the circle there is a large bead, on which the Lord's Prayer is said. Then come ten small beads for ten Hail Marys. The next large bead is used for the Gloria, which concludes the first decade, and for the Lord's Prayer, which begins the next. There are thus five decades around the circle. You exit back down the pendant (as above but in reverse order).

The saying of these prayers is combined with a pattern of 15 meditations on subjects drawn from the life of Jesus, and devotion to his mother Mary. These subjects are known as 'mysteries' and fall into three groups: five Joyful Mysteries, five Sorrowful Mysteries and five Glorious Mysteries. As each decade of the rosary is said one of these subjects is meditated on so that each time the complete five decades of the rosary is prayed one of the three groups of mysteries is worked through.

In order to deepen your meditations, you will probably want to reflect on each of the mysteries outside of your time of prayer, studying the relevant Bible passages where appropriate.

There is no reason why you could not use other words if you wanted to, substituting the Jesus Prayer or some other simple biblical phrase for the Hail Mary. Equally, you could choose a different set of Glorious Mysteries if you wanted to use only biblical subjects.

Or you could simply use a string of beads as something you hold, and move along from one bead to the next while praying. It might or might not be helpful quietly to say a word or phrase that is meaningful to you as you move from one bead to the next.

Hail Mary

'Hail Mary, full of grace; the Lord is with thee; blessed art thou among women and blessed is the fruit of thy womb, Jesus. Holy Mary, Mother of God, pray for us sinners now and at the hour of our death. Amen.'

Gloria

'Glory be to the Father, and to the Son, and to the Holy Spirit. As it was in the beginning, is now and ever shall be. Amen.'

Joyful Mysteries

1 The Annunciation (Luke 1.26–38)
2 Mary visits Elizabeth (Luke 1.39–42)
3 The Nativity (Luke 2.4–8)
4 The Presentation in the Temple (Luke 2.22–25)
5 The Finding of Jesus in the Temple (Luke 2.46–49)

Sorrowful Mysteries

1 The Agony in the Garden (Luke 22.39–46)
2 The Scourging (Mark 15.9–15)
3 Jesus is crowned with thorns (Matthew 27.27–31)
4 Jesus carries his cross (John 19.16–19)
5 The Crucifixion (Luke 23.44–47)

Glorious Mysteries

1 The Resurrection (Matthew 28.5–8)
2 The Ascension (Luke 24.50–53)
3 The Coming of the Holy Spirit (Acts 2.1–5)
4 The Assumption
5 The Coronation of the Virgin (Revelation 11.19; 12.1–2)

HM

When 'God language' breaks down

I have a priest friend with whom I have been meeting regularly for many years to reflect together on his journey with God. One day when we met he said that he thought that perhaps this would be our last meeting. I asked him why, and he replied that the theistic framework was no longer helpful to him: to ask, 'Where is God in all this?' was no longer helpful or indeed meaningful.

I replied that it seemed to me that while this might be the right time to end our meetings, it might equally be argued that this was precisely the time when we should continue, as he was now facing the possibility of considerable change in his way of thinking about life. We agreed to continue to meet, and I was especially glad that we did so because it became clear in conversation that he felt a sense of rejection from a number of his other Christian friends because of his newly found position.

If the question, 'Where is God in all this?' is no longer a helpful one to ask, what might be a helpful alternative question, I asked him. We came up with three possibilities:

Is life purposeful or meaningful?
Is life wholesome?
What are the quality of my relationships?

When we meet now these questions are where we start our conversations.

I've mentioned this conversation with many people over the years and have noted some alternative questions they have identified. You might like to reflect on some of them yourself, not least because trying to frame and answer these questions without resort to overtly religious language sometimes brings interesting insights to light, and can lead us to see things with a new clarity.

What is the meaning of life?
Does my lifestyle support this meaning?
Where and when does meaning break into my life?
What are the issues against which the meaning is currently being tested?
What inspires me to go on living?
What gives me life?
What brings disintegration and death?
What do I ultimately hope for?
Where do I see energy in the world?
To whom do I give thanks?
What expletive might I use in the face of a disaster?
What question is life asking me now?

All this raises a number of interesting questions for me. I think that there are many people who struggle, as my friend does, with 'God language'. Now it may be that these people have rejected any notion of belief in God. But it seems to me equally possible that what they have rejected is not God but the language we use about God. I recall a quote from Simone Weil: 'There are two atheisms of which one is a purification of the notion of God' (in Miller, 1967). What I understand this to mean is that we may no longer believe in God, or we may continue to believe but reject most, perhaps all, of the language we have grown accustomed to using about God. This may be a terrifying experience, but it might also be a purifying of our knowledge of God.

Rationally, this is not very surprising. By definition, God is bound to be beyond our understanding. So any language we use about God, however useful and true it may be, must to some extent become an idol standing in the way of the full truth about God, in which case a little purification of our language might be a very good idea. To realize this, and to reject the language, may actually be a great *act* of faith rather than a *rejection* of faith. All of which suggests to me that the line between faith and atheism is often a very fine one, and may be difficult for us to discern. Someone may sound like an atheist but in fact have a deep faith, and someone else may sound like a person of faith but in fact be using faith as a way of avoiding an encounter with the true God. We therefore do well to proceed carefully and to refrain from judgement.

So we should be careful in our use of language about God, and especially beware of dumping the language that currently helps us on to other people. Many people, I suspect, when they 'reject' God, are not in reality rejecting God at all: they are reacting against and rejecting language about God which they hear believers claiming to be the only legitimate language to use, but which they cannot accept because it doesn't match their own experience and they don't find it helpful. I sometimes wonder if our evangelism may not put more people off than it helps? As I'm not against evangelism in principle, I'm not quite sure where I go with that. Perhaps we should heed the words of St Francis of Assisi: 'Preach the gospel at all times, and if all else fails use words.'

A difficulty is that when you let go of 'God language' it is not at all clear where you go instead. What other language might do? What if no language seems right? Often people move from this position into silence or music or images or nature, and somewhat to their surprise they find that God is there already waiting for them!

HM

Part 3

THE STORIES OTHERS TELL

11

God in our passions

Introduction

I suggested in Chapter 2 that the biblical witness is that God can and does speak to us through anything and everything. If everything is God's creation then everything will have God's 'thumbprint' on it and it is therefore hardly surprising that we can find God in everything if we have the eyes to see.

I also suggested that we often seem to find it easier to hear God speaking to us when we are doing things that we enjoy, things that we are committed to and passionate about. Again, this is not perhaps very surprising because when we are enjoying ourselves we are probably more likely to be relaxed and open, and therefore more receptive to God. A corollary is that time for pleasure needs to be a part of our spiritual discipline. Many Christians find this a difficult pill to swallow. Some have been brought up with the notion that if you are enjoying yourself then it can't be good for you. But if God is a loving God who seeks a relationship founded on love with us, who has created the world and sees it as good, then enjoying God's creation and being open to God's presence in the process sounds like a virtue it's hard to find fault with.

We can put this another way. If we pay attention to what we are passionate about, to what gives us pleasure (providing, of course, that it isn't something that does harm to ourselves, others or the planet) then it will have much to teach us about life and will inevitably end up leading us to God.

I learnt this for myself as a teenager standing on the terraces at White Hart Lane watching my beloved Spurs play football. Football was and still is one of my abiding passions. A hitherto untapped part of me came alive amid the crowd of 50,000 people supporting our team, cheering when they played well and groaning when things went badly (an experience not unlike attending a Pentecostal meeting, I used to suspect). It was in the camaraderie of the invariably good-hearted crowd that I discovered myself to be part of some corporate something bigger than me. Like every true football supporter I gave my commitment to my team, and once it's given that commitment can never be taken back. I read once in a magazine that English men are statistically more likely to seek a divorce from an unsatisfactory marriage than they are to stop supporting their football team when it is playing badly. That's very, very sad but I fear that it's true! I am forever a Spurs supporter and my mood on a Saturday night was, and still is somewhat to my embarrassment, largely determined by how the lads have got on in the afternoon. I have no control over this. My mood depends on what happens to a group of men over whom I have no control whatsoever. Football teaches me to cope with the glorious highs of success as well as the sloughs of despond and failure. Hope springs eternal at the beginning of each new season, and every match is a fresh start. This is not unlike the Christian life, I used to think, for once I was committed to belief in God I soon realized that I was not in charge of my life any more, and I had to learn to roll with what comes.

On a good day when the team are playing well it's all poetry and art, but when things aren't going so well you have to roll your sleeves up, get stuck in, and just do your best to grind out a result: life's a lot like that too!

Back in those teenage years one of Spurs' great rivals were Wolves, who played a rather more physical style of football. An image is etched on my memory from a night game against them. It was billed as a crucial clash of two giants of the game, and the outcome was said to hinge on whether the Spurs midfield creative genius, a Scot called Johnny White, could evade the shackles that the hard-tackling Wolves defender Ron Flowers would seek to place on him. Spurs broke out of defence on their left and play moved quickly down their left flank. Johnny White raced from the left side of the pitch away from where the ball was, into the large open spaces of the right side of the pitch. This looked like complete madness; he appeared to be running away from the play. But it was in fact a stroke of genius; he was putting himself into space from which the ball was switched for him to deliver a killer pass.

I have learnt more from that image about life and my relationship with God than from countless sermons and talks. I learnt young that my passion was my teacher in life and a sure path to God. Listening over the years to friends talking about their passions, I realized that what was true for me seemed to be equally true for others. So in this chapter I have invited a number of friends to reflect on their passions and what they have learnt from them, and whether or not they might have led them deeper into God.

This chapter clearly cannot cover all possible passions, but tries to offer a range of them. Some of these passions you may have experienced personally, but you may reflect differently on them, others may be new to you. We are not suggesting that these contributions offer *the* way to reflect on these activities, but that they offer *a* way. Hopefully these ways will stimulate deeper and renewed reflection on your own experience. You might like to write a piece on your passion for your own personal benefit. And if you'd like to send it by email to Roy and myself (see <www.annunciationtrust.org.uk/>) we'll be pleased to consider adding it to the Annunciation Trust website for others to read and perhaps be inspired by.

A final thought. If our passions lead us to God, whether they be football, singing, dancing or whatever, these are activities that large numbers of people indulge in, most of whom have no explicit Christian faith. But if we recognize that God meets us there, then presumably God meets all these other punters there too. Maybe they name and recognize God in what they are doing. Maybe they don't. I'm not sure how much that matters. Didn't Jesus say something to the effect that it's not those who say 'Lord, Lord' who will enter the kingdom of heaven, but those who do the will of his Father in heaven? Maybe naming God is less important than being in touch with God and responding to the God who is actively in touch with us. And it appears that the God we are dealing with is a God who meets us in whatever we are passionate about and who touches us there. Who are we to pass judgement on how others respond to that touch? How can we possibly tell?

HM

Patchwork

OK, so maybe a passion for patchwork seems a little odd, cutting up bits of material in order to sew them together again! But then, there's probably something a little strange to the outsider about most passions. Patchwork is my passion; it's about working with colour, pattern and texture. It's being creative, getting involved in making something new: it energizes me. I love the feel of fabric and look for beautifully coloured and patterned cottons for quilting, although sometimes I'll use other materials to bring in light or dark, or just because I want to bend the rules a bit further, or attempt the impossible once again . . . Sometimes I'll get a different feeling by altering the surface of the cloth, folding it, putting in pleats and tucks that move the fabric here and there, giving depth and texture.

Quilting allows me to be reflective: with my hands occupied my mind is freer to dip and dive, making connections. Traditional patchwork is about repeating blocks, laid out so that an overall pattern flows across them. One block on its own may look nothing much, but together they sing a completely different song. There's a rhythm and a flow to this repetition of pattern that feels like good liturgy; it feeds the soul, stilling it so that God can be heard and encountered in a new way. Occasionally, when prayer becomes impossible, quilting becomes my only way of connecting with God. When life is difficult, I leave frustration behind as I quilt. When things are going well, I glory in being creative. Either way, I have to quilt, and ignoring that passion leaves me in dangerous waters, where I am somehow less 'myself'.

There's a real energy in starting a new quilt, as there can be in starting anything new. As a child I was taught to always finish things, but I've learnt not to worry overmuch about unfinished quilting projects: either a flash of an idea will transform them, or they will be unsuccessful experiments to shelve or abandon. Quilting has helped me appreciate the importance of community. Historically, quilts were often group efforts, an almost subversive form of artistic expression by women who had few other outlets for their creativity. And the sense of the quilting community is still strong. I've found quilt groups to be very friendly, cooperative groups of people, always willing to share ideas and often working together.

Most quilts use only the simplest of stitches, just a running stitch, but the simple can become divine in the hands of the creator with imagination. Quilting can speak of resurrection. Recycling might be a modern catchword, but quilters have always recycled fabric inventively, resurrecting the new from the old. Even the tiniest fragments of fabric can be used in quilting; all have a contribution to make, something that enriches, just as our simple actions can together bring about the kingdom of God.

But quilting takes time and patience – both often difficult to find. Sometimes people ask me how long it takes to make a quilt: it can be years, but most of the time is spent thinking and dreaming my way towards finishing, trying new ideas, ripping out stitches that don't work, or are inaccurate – a slow process. In a world obsessed by words, quilting communicates in a different way, drawing ideas outside the straitjacket of words. I'm often surprised by what people see in my quilts, but one thing quilting teaches me is always to be open to being surprised!

Annabel Barber

Singing

A bit late, you might think – I discovered my passion for singing in my mid-fifties. You'd be partly right – many singing avenues are closed to me through my late start; my body is simply too old to adapt in the ways necessary for a high-flying singer. That has been and is a source of deep grief – and anger: towards God and others who might have pointed me in the right direction and encouraged me when I was young, and towards myself for being so fearful for all those years.

But one of the many lessons of my life-journey of faith and learning is to grow by putting the regrets into the background. They don't go away, I know they are there, but I am determined to make the most of life as it is, with what I have, now. The God of my childhood and earlier life, micromanaging the details of the world scene and my personal life, has gone. I, in company with travelling companions, have the responsibility for what I make of my gifts and circumstances.

So now I sing when I can and I love it. The hard work of choir rehearsals is richly rewarded in performance. Occasionally an unsought moment of transcendence is the 'icing on the cake'. I can still feel the thrill of the first concert during which this happened, in Vaughan Williams' *Serenade to Music*. Then it's hard to hold back the emotions and concentrate on the next few bars. There's nothing like it! In these moments, I am drawn out of myself towards the transcendent, the energy holding everything together, the creative force – call it God if you like, but I'm still working on throwing away the unwanted connotations accompanying that title.

Patricia Price-Tomes

Picture framing

The Vincent Van Gogh museum in Amsterdam is a marvellous tribute to one of the great artists. It also helps me explain why I enjoy picture framing. Poor in his lifetime, Vincent (1853–90) sold very little of his work and relied on his brother Theo to support him. In the gallery you will see two extremes of framing. The first is a study of the colour yellow called *Still Life with Quinces and Lemons* (1887–88). It is moving because it is bordered by the only original painted frame made by Van Gogh himself. No others have been preserved. There are gaps in the corners of the frame and the painted wood is chipped and faded in places. The frame would never pass a trade exam and yet it has a symmetry, simplicity and beauty all of its own. This work is displayed alongside the second extreme; other masterpieces since placed in incredibly ornate, exquisite and beautifully gilded frames. These surround and proclaim the works of a grand master. Some of them in fact are so ornate they almost detract from the artwork! As an amateur framer wandering this famous gallery I found myself itching to reframe many of the paintings to better complement the artwork.

Picture framing is an intricate, detailed and fascinating industry. I first became interested in it when I had a sabbatical from my day job as a vicar. I wanted to do something practical and different, so I attended a professional framing course. This week-long residential course was great fun and totally absorbing. The hours from morning to night flew by and at the end I had produced seven pictures framed to a high standard, and learnt a great deal from our tutor. I resolved to continue, and along with a developing interest in art, I was hooked, and sensed God's hand leading my enthusiasm. In my life this has been a hard lesson. I have had to learn that God can guide me through my passions and interests outside of the church. In this case I'm glad I did respond by continuing a new-found hobby. It is one I never dreamt I would follow as I never learnt about art at school and only had rudimentary woodwork lessons. However, it is now an important part of my life and teaches me a great deal about discipline, care and preparation as well as appreciating a craft.

I enjoy framing because of the sense of completeness it gives. To work with a beautiful piece of art, a print, or simply a favourite family picture, is deeply satisfying and, for me, has become a form of prayer. I now have a mini workshop with much of the equipment professionals will use. I can easily engross myself in the workshop, as each new project is a fresh challenge and allows me to be creative and detailed in a way my everyday experience of life does not. Taking a picture I have first to plan the frame. I have to make design decisions, which can't easily be changed later. I then have to carry out the work, cutting mounts, mouldings and glass. This can be a painstaking process since each stage requires great care and some skill. I make mistakes and these can be costly in time and money, and at times the work can even be very frustrating. But, I liken all of this to my spiritual journey with God. It too needs planning, there can be times of enormous creativity and there can also be immensely frustrating times. However, at the end of the process is a beautiful changed object. Framing adds value and can enhance work that otherwise may have little significance. Similarly God changes me, and framing quality art well, and enjoying it, is helpful to my discovery of him. Every time I look at a piece of work I can have a conversation with God about its beauty and how it may be used for his purposes.

I am a bit further on now and am interested in skills like gilding and bespoke work. Every time I visit a gallery I explore the work on show and the way it is displayed and framed. I learn from looking and talking to others and I have come across some new and fascinating people who care about art, conservation and producing the best of work. All this speaks to me of the creativity of God and the beauty of the world around us, not just that inside a church building but also in the art gallery and beyond.

John Fisher

Wood carving

I am passionate about wood carving. I began by making board and table games. I then made a cot, and toys for a growing family. While I quickly came to love the feel and the smell of the wood, all this was using wood for my own purposes.

I then tried my hand at carving, and found something different began to happen: the shape of the piece of wood, and the way the grain revealed itself as I worked it with a plane or a gouge, began to influence or even dictate what I was making. There was a sense of revealing what was already present, but hidden.

This speaks to me of how we human beings interact with creation. We sometimes sense a presence beyond the physical experience of our surroundings. It can be as if something out there is reaching towards us, a spiritual presence with which we can cooperate. Religious people may use the word 'God' of this, or spell 'spirit' with a capital 'S'; many would not do that, and yet the experience itself seems widespread, far beyond people who are overtly religious.

An example of this process happening is a series of carvings I made in response to the music of Arvo Pärt's *Magnificat Antiphons*. These antiphons were short sentences sung by the monks and nuns on the days leading up to Christmas, a different antiphon each day. A form of them is familiar to people who go to church in the words of the hymn, 'O come, O come Emmanuel'. But while the hymn has a chorus, 'Rejoice . . .', the original antiphons constitute a prayer, 'O come . . .'. Arvo Pärt is an Estonian. His country suffered terribly at the hands of a ruthless atheistic Soviet regime until it gained independence in 1991. His music therefore has a desperation to it, which still feels appropriate to many of the troubled places of the world: 'O Daystar . . . come and enlighten those who dwell in darkness and the shadow of death.'

I decided to use slabs of spalted beech on which to carve a symbol of each antiphon, the symbol in each case surrounded by an 'O', all of them made to stand in a circle or arc. As I worked on the wood, I found that the markings in the grain could illustrate the meaning. Not only did the letters of 'Oriens' (Daystar) form an 'O' with rays coming out from it, the marking in the grain emerged as a burst of light, like a photograph of a distant galaxy. But some things I discovered only later. After carving them I visited the Outer Hebrides and Orkney, and realized I had made the slabs in the shape of the standing stones of Calanais or the Ring of Brodgar, with all their mysterious associations. Somebody then pointed out that the symbol in the 'O' was a cartouche, an ancient Egyptian symbol for a god. And almost every time I use these, and other carvings, with music, in a form of meditation others will point out meanings that had never occurred to me.

So carving wood is, for me, a way God speaks not only to me, but through the carving to others also, in ways that can be intensely moving.

Christopher Lewis

(Christopher Lewis has written a book about his passion. It has colour photographs of 22 of his carvings and offers thoughts on all of them. See References, page 222.)

Cooking

I am passionate about food! Not just stuffing my face – although I do love eating. No, it's the preparation and cooking of food that is my special passion.

'Trust your instincts' is a good rule of thumb for cooking. If the first principle is 'use the best, freshest ingredients', then the second must be 'taste it as you go'. Taste buds are the best judge of character where food is concerned. As a lover of food I instinctively know when it is well prepared and cooked – so that it will nourish not only body but soul.

It is much the same as a lover of God instinctively knowing the nourishment of the Spirit; 'Taste and see that the Lord is good,' says the psalmist. I have intuitively learnt to trust my instincts. For me, cooking and preparing food puts me in touch with a God who cares about nourishing me as a whole person; not only my spiritual, but my physical, emotional and mental being is of infinite value to God.

Whether the food I work with is vegan, vegetarian or includes meat and fish, when I cook I am collaborating with the earth – the land that produces the raw materials of our diet. Cooking engages me with the created world, and with the creator.

Why am I passionate about food, and how does it energize my spirit? Cooking for me is a creative thing. I am energized when I create a meal out of some gathered ingredients, just as others may be working with wood or clay. Cooking connects me with the creator God in whose creative image I am made. I am more truly myself when I am engaging with food and cooking it. Even a cup of coffee is a work of art for me! 'Coffee boiled is coffee spoiled' is a mantra I heard years ago and remember, and it rings in my ears whenever I'm near a cafetière!

There is no doubt in my mind that there is a spiritual dimension to food. In many cultures it is around food that interpersonal relationships develop, communication flows, and hospitality is extended. In British culture, this has traditionally focused around the dinner table, either in the middle of the day, when shops and offices closed down for an hour or so to honour the importance of the 'meal time', or in the evening. There is something 'sacred' for me about meeting around the table.

In other cultures, it is not only the meal itself that is sacred, but also the preparation and cooking of that meal. In Morocco, for example, the preparing of the fire and the food, the placing of the food in the tagine (a pot with a tall, funnel-like lid, resembling a clay wigwam), and the tending of the tagine and fire until the meal is ready are as much a focus of extended family relationships, and hospitality, as the eating of the meal together.

That whole concept which gathers together food, conversation, relationship and hospitality thrills my spirit and sends a tingle down my spine! Show me food, a kitchen, a table and I become lost in creativity. It teaches me that God can take the simplest of ingredients and create something wonderful. It reminds me that all of our senses are involved in the life of the spirit; smell, taste and texture are all ways in which we can sense God.

There are some cooking techniques that teach me about God too. Meat is so much more tender if it is marinated well – it needs time to infuse, as I need to give time for infusion in God if I am to become a tender person. Much baking needs air, and not to be overworked if it is to be light. I, too, can become stodgy without adequate airspace, and when I allow myself to be overworked. A cook's knife needs to be sharpened each time it is used; it cannot rely on being a 'good knife', or the fact that it was sharp last time! Similarly I find I cannot afford to become complacent or I become blunt, tearing through life rather than living it with the respect and honour that food, well prepared, cooked and eaten embodies.

Paul Booth

Hospitality

I've always enjoyed cooking. It was a revelation to me when I discovered that I could actually cook, and if you followed a recipe the finished product looked passably like the one illustrated in the cookbook. I thought it was a kind of magic. In the early days, of course, cooking was an activity that *had* to be done. I had a young family at the time and cooked for them and although it was always enjoyable it was constrained by set times and the particular likes and dislikes of my brood.

However, I also enjoyed having my friends round for light relief and we would always have a meal together. After a while I dove-tailed the two things and my sons had the same meal as my guests but probably at an earlier time. My greatest delight has been in recent years when I have entertained friends for the sheer pleasure of doing it, and when my sons became the honoured guests at the meal, together with their own families. In their turn they have always enjoyed entertaining me by cooking for me, so there has been a direct spin-off.

I like to have the house prepared for entertaining, and I try to make sure there is a relaxing atmosphere, preferably with candlelight and I always have some good music on. I never cook anything I haven't tried on myself first several times so that I can almost cook it without thinking. I always have plenty of wine and cream around. I like to make sure there is plenty of everything. Then I sit back and enjoy people and the food. There's no better combination. Just being able to have that time with people, that space together to sit and linger in each other's company over an enjoyable meal and something good to drink is sheer joy. Moments like that are all too few in an age where we are rushing to get things done and where most of our activities in an age of computer technology are solitary.

Enjoying each other, and taking time to do so, really listening to each other's stories and sharing each other's joys and sorrows is for me part of treasuring people.

I think feeding people is pretty basic; it's about caring and nur-turing and I suppose as a mother those instincts linger on in me and are translated into the world at large. Entertaining people, giving them hospitality, is about giving them a space to be themselves and to really 'be'. It's about making them feel valued and respected and welcome. For me there is the delight in making it happen.

I think God invites us to sit and eat with him and be his friends. To take time out from our busyness and just enjoy him is not just a rewarding thing for us to do; I think it also delights God. I was struck by the fact the other day that whereas I send out an invitation for a particular day at a particular time so that I can make sure everything is ready, God operates an open house all the time, his generosity is far wider than we could ever possibly imagine, and he always has the time.

Lydia Wells

Photography

I have noticed that photographs move me emotionally in a way that other visual art does not. I cannot find an explanation but I am content to notice the phenomenon and see that it is a way that God gets my attention towards people, situations and creation. I can lose myself in framing photographs, which brings me to a place of peace, joy and attention to the 'now' which for me is prayer. The process of doing this and taking the photographs I find engages me with the world in a way that few other things do.

It is a form of creativity that brings me satisfaction, since I take images out of a necessity in me to 'slow down and look'. It is nice when the photographs are appreciated by others, but that is not what they are for and is very much the 'icing on the cake'.

I find that I am captivated by a personal impact of an image that seems to vary in content but gives me a sense of wonder, interest or sheer delight. This can be places, people, things or patterns and is somewhat unpredictable. I have noticed that narrative or story for me is an important part of an image and I enjoy choosing titles for my work. I enjoy mornings, evenings and trees, which I find often come together to make a romantic or spiritual theme.

I like to visit places where there is 'space and light' and people, and then take a large number of images to capture the feel of the place. I recently spent time at the new St Pancras Station in London and particularly around the statue of a couple embracing, which sums up the 'feel' of stations and the life and relationships that are dramatically seen there. I attempted to take an image that captured the largeness of the station, the individuality of the shoes and the sense of dressing up to go to Paris, which are all part of that statue.

131

Another image, of my grandchild taken at a carnival, was not premeditated but came out of enjoying a day with my family and just 'snapping' with an automatic as I took part in the joy of the afternoon.

Recently I tried to communicate the finding of a simple pleasure on a wet summer afternoon. The image uses the light-reflecting water and the freedom and delight of a child's approach to a muddy puddle in wellington boots.

A further aspect of image that I try to convey is the unusual or amusing, giving a new view of reality or one that is unexpected. I often use silhouettes in images, which emphasize the beauty and drama of shapes, particularly trees. Photography leads me to spend time with the unnoticed, the surprising, and to see beauty in the little things as well as the great dramas of creation made by light and shade. Images lead me back to God and a childlike astonishment and wonder at the beauty of the world and its peoples.

RG

Living without a goal?

It was a moment of compelling absurdity. There I was, a windswept young Englishman perched on the terrace steps of a small-time Scottish football ground (the romantically named Boghead Park), suddenly caught up in a frenzy of yelling, whooping and embracing. Just the kind of unfettered emotion that in other circumstances would probably have caused me acute embarrassment.

This scene, minus the socialized inhibition, is hardly unusual. You will find its equivalent in sporting arenas across the world any weekend. But for me a first half goal by Dumbarton striker Peter Houston, scored on 5 September 1987, was pure epiphany. The team I had been irrationally supporting from a distance of 400 miles for nearly 18 years had finally hit the net in my presence, following a dozen goal-free afternoons stretched over many months of anticipation-ending-in-emptiness.

The fact that it turned out to be a pretty scrappy consolation goal struck in a dreary lower division match against Hamilton

Accies, which we had already lost 2–1 before the break, really didn't matter to me. My previously goalless life suddenly felt strangely complete in an incident of ecstatic insignificance.

Well, as they say – go figure. The bemused 'Sons' supporters standing around me looked slightly taken aback by this weird Sassenach suddenly going wild about something that surely only merited a quick burst of applause before the return of a few dozen pairs of hands to the doleful pockets that were their rightful domain.

But this was and is football. A strange cocktail of artistry, industry, geometry and (much of the time) drudgery which, for those of us who find ourselves hooked, mirrors life's ups and downs but also renders them sensible to an athletic period drama, a few reams of statistics and a particular repository of dreams. That is, you and me. But really, wonders my eminently sensible spouse, what's the point?

Here's one take on that. The best definition of prayer I have ever come across, and certainly the one that has made most sense to my own 50 years of muddling experience, is 'learning to waste time with God'. (A bit like learning to waste time with 22 men and a lump of leather, maybe? Well, OK, perhaps I'm stretching that one.)

In a world where we are encouraged to acquire money, to ration time and pursue attainment from cradle to grave, liberating spirituality (as distinct from the consumer kind that has become a synonym for 'personal development') means letting go of one's illusions about control and cultivating unexpected joys.

Those nameless occasions which I get to call prayer, football, music or art: they show me something about the world that enables me to realize that nothing can manufacture the true experience of grace, elation, love, completeness and transcendence. These things just are, and in 'just being' they speak of something precious beyond bargaining and calculation. God's life overflowing into ours, one might say. And I would.

Passion such as one feels with the first chord of a symphony, the final whistle of a match or a lover's incidental touch knows no boundary between sacred and profane, religious and secular. Such things can pass you by, or they can change your life. They can fill time or fulfil it. Alarmingly, their impact or lack of it depends on you rather than on anything magical in the air. Times of inexplicable intensity can prepare you for even more, for sharing and multiplying. But only with practice . . . the practice of letting go and letting be.

This, for me, is not a way of becoming that I can think myself into. It is a state of sheer gift: an epiphenomenon of the rub of the turf or the jink of the ball. With music, my other 'balancing passion' (as I describe it, along with football, in my 'potted biography'), it is possible, in a certain way, to reappropriate life-giving moments through repeat performance. In sport they are, technically, unrepeatable. Yet they go on happening. That is the God-born world that prayer invites us to see. Living without a goal, yet finding them all the time.

Simon Barrow

Modern art

One of my favourite places is the Musée D'Orsay in Paris. I've only been twice, but both times my breath was taken away by the artworks on display. One particular painting has an extraordinary effect on me. I am a priest in the Church of England. I value works of art and have always appreciated religious work in particular. I am also a fan of the great impressionist artist Vincent Van Gogh. The museum has a few of his famous works including The Church at Auvers-sur-Oise (1890, oil on canvas). You would probably recognize the picture if you saw a reproduction of it, as it is so famous. On my first visit I expected to be transfixed by this scene. However, imagine my surprise when I was utterly captivated by another Van Gogh nearby, and not the religious subject. Instead, Thatches at Cordeville, at Auvers-sur-Oise (1890, oil on canvas) kept drawing me to look at it. I had to go back several times and fight my way through crowds to do it! The picture is important to me and even now the feeling I experienced stays with me with profound depth. You may ask why. What was so important and why the lasting effect? Let me try to explain.

An artist friend of mine, Mark Cazalet, often quotes Paul Klee in saying that 'artists make visible the invisible'. In other words, they interpret the world by capturing the ordinary in whatever media they use, thereby giving it significance. They might see beauty, or they might see controversy. They might wish to convey a message, or they might simply rejoice in the creative process for its own sake. Whatever the motive behind their work, artists have ideas and something to say, but not usually in words. Now I am not an artist! I don't paint, draw or sculpt. I have tried and found it very difficult. However, I love art and I have a great respect for artists who seek to make their living from the profession, but do so without compromising their artistic integrity and ideals. I take great pleasure in viewing their work and meeting the individuals involved. I find it a stimulating world emotionally and intellectually and, as a person of faith, I find art an incredibly productive spiritual ground. I need to spend time going to exhibitions, reading the reviews and teaching myself more. There is much art in my own Christian tradition, which I affirm and appreciate, but I have found a purely religious approach too restricting and this is where my experience with *Thatches at Cordeville* is significant. It is a swirling landscape with heavy brushstrokes and beautiful colouring. It takes an ordinary village scene and fills it with wonder, life and vitality. It oozes spiritual energy and as I look I can lose myself and meet God through the vision of Van Gogh. An ordinary scene becomes an explosion of beauty and a powerful affirmation of the world. It lifts my spirits to the divine and renews my hope in the world.

Nowadays I can often find out more about God and the world by looking at contemporary art. For me contemporary artists are like the prophets of the Old Testament in the Bible. They can disturb, provoke or upset. They can appreciate, rejoice and praise. Most of all they are never static, but critique society (including the Church) and call us all to account. There are many gifted artists at work (including artists of faith) and through them I can discover God, often outside the boundaries of the church building.

John Fisher

Gardening

My earliest and happiest memories include plants and flowers on my grandparents' dairy farm where I was born. Aged two or three, lying among buttercups and grasses on a Sunday morning, hearing church bells above the buzzing of insects, and instinctively sensing that I was more in touch with God and the spiritual there than in the strange though familiar service I would shortly be obliged to sit through. A sense of belonging, security, at-homeness and oneness with the natural world, which I lost later but found again when I needed it most. The spicy scent of phlox in the garden mingling with the heavy ripeness of Victoria plums and dozy wasps. The pure whiteness and shape of arum lilies, and delving among the strawberry plants for forbidden fruits while inhaling the sweet smell of summer jasmine growing along the wall. Good memories of things that fed my very young soul along with the gentle cows and calves, hens, pigs, dogs and cat.

In later years I followed and watched my parents who were gardeners and in my adult years it came naturally to me to garden and find great pleasure in growing and tending plants.

I have discovered that all the lessons of life are contained in the natural world and husbandry if I open my inner ears and eyes and give time to reflection. Through gardening I am in touch with conception, birth, growth, sickness and disease, dying, death and resurrection and through the sowing of seeds, bulbs and plants I learn about clearing the ground, good preparation, appropriate nurturing, patient waiting with hope, excitement and delight as well as disappointment and despair. Bulbs buried for eight or nine months of the year before the green noses above the soil teach me about the 'dark night of the soul'; to trust and rest in the ongoing work of the Spirit within though all is experienced as darkness and loss. I learn that some plants need hard pruning to bring out their best while others respond to some gentle cosseting, although all need to 'stand on their own two feet'. Most flourish if surrounded by others to provide a healthy environment but with enough space, light and moisture to develop their unique character. And of course, it's no good planting lavender in damp, heavy clay or expecting hostas to flower well in hot, sandy soil, though there is always the exception to the rule, if only for a short time!

If we image God as the ground – the soil, humus of our being – we need to have our roots in close contact in order to receive nourishment, so watering, feeding, replenishing and weeding, or their spiritual equivalent, are important. I could continue for many pages!

But I learn too of the interdependence of all living things, so I do not use chemicals, and plant with awareness of the needs of wildlife. I love my compost heaps and bonfires and thank God for worms! Most of the snails are sacrificed to the thrushes, but slugs! Well, slugs, although the gardener's enemy, are gourmet delight for hedgehogs. I feel a lesson in non-attachment lurks in there somewhere!

All these lessons! Is that all it is about? No, of course not. Gardening keeps me in touch with the miraculous, the ongoing cycle of life through the seasons, the sun and moon, and every sort of weather. I work deeply aware of the Source of Life and in cooperation with her through Mother Earth. Each year I watch in awe as the runner bean plants rampage over the canes producing hundreds of bright orange flowers and then, lo, there are beans which I cook and eat. And all from small kidney-shape seeds planted in the soil earlier. Every year I experience wonder and a deep-down delight as the snowdrops appear, green shoots push through the earth and young leaves are born. I remember a time of great depression in my life when there seemed no point in life continuing. I went for a winter walk and stood in the snow under a beech tree. After a while my eyes focused on the branches and I noticed the already forming buds of the new leaves. I saw in my mind the strong roots going down into the earth, continuing to nourish the life of the tree during the cold, dark winter months, and felt warmth in my heart.

And now as I wander around or sit quietly watching the birds and butterflies, inhaling the scents and enjoying the beautiful shapes, textures and colours, my heart is warmed again for they speak to me of God's love, compassion and delight in all of creation, including me. And I am given peace, courage, hope and the grace to continue the gardening of my own soul in cooperation with my Maker.

Sylvia Morgan

Hills and moors

I am passionate about hills and moors. I'm drawn to them, love to be among them, looking at them, on them – and I feel close to God when I am: they lift my soul. Some people find great expanses of moorland frightening and threatening but I just love them – those wide open spaces unlock the door-catch of my heart and set me free.

I'm sitting writing this high up on the North Yorkshire moors in August – the sky is mainly a dark grey but the sun has just come out and is setting alight the deep purple of the heather that stretches as far as my eye can see. Earlier this afternoon I was walking on a track over these same moors, alone but not alone – a female wheatear, a bright green caterpillar, a lone curlew – and who knows what else, who else? It was quiet, no abstractions, 'the mind's cession of its kingdom' (R. S. Thomas, from 'The Moor').

And when I'm up – on a hill, on the moors – my eyes are constantly drawn to the distant horizon, to the limit of what I can see, straining to see beyond. Is this the pull of the infinite one, the God who has no name but who is ever present – transcendent and yet immanent?

The urge to see beyond is complemented by my fascination with what is under my feet – the shape of the rocks, the plants and flowers, the feel of the earth, the heather, the grass under my boots – connecting, grounded, earthed. And if it rains, that is a challenge – there is something elemental about being out there experiencing the raw caress of God's creation.

I remember once being with friends up Glen Sligachan on Skye, surrounded and enveloped by the high peaks of the Cuillins. It was wet, and I was not alone, but there was such a sense of stillness, of being held – it was unforgettable – like being hugged and held close within the love of God.

Is it the shape of the hills and their surroundings that I love so much? I think so – the hidden valleys, the little hillocks, the sweep of the hillsides perhaps dotted with a barn or a white farmstead or a lone tree – sheer poetry writ large on an immense canvas: 'What is man that you are mindful of him?' (Psalm 8.4, NIV).

And best of all, I love the long, flat-topped moors and hills of the Yorkshire dales and moors where it looks as if I could walk for miles and miles, free, unfettered, my heart singing praises to God – Wordsworth's 'a sense sublime of something far more deeply interfused' – part of my whole being, and a source of energy and creativity.

And then there's the light – something I have come to enjoy, value and delight in more and more as I have got older. It is never the same – constantly changing – the sunlight on the hills, the lowering clouds, the rainbows, the light of dawn when I get up early to watch the black grouse lek, the bright midday shimmering light, the evening light as the shadows lengthen and deepen. It is all so indescribably beautiful that it brings tears to my eyes. I can't get enough of it – I just want to 'gaze and gaze on Thee'.

I love people and could not live without them, but I need to go to the hills. There is a stability about them, although they do change – the light and the seasons see to that – but I am not in control of that. I am a watcher, an admirer – and I watch in wonder and in awe.

For me the glory of God is manifest all around us, not just in creation. But for me it is the hills and moors that enlarge my heart, attune my soul to the infinite, refresh me, put the concerns of my little life back in perspective – take my focus from a centre that is me to God who is the true centre of my life, 'so that we may evermore dwell in Him and He in us'.

Ruth Stables

A walk on the wild side

I recently went for a post-Easter break to the north-west coast of Scotland to do some walking. After a good pint of An Tealloch one evening, I decided that the mountain of that name was worth exploring. Ever since a Youth Hostels Association trip to Snowdonia when I was 15, mountains have held a fascination. They are dangerous places, and they are beautiful. From a great height, you can look down on the world, and yet feel how tiny a speck you are in the immensity of rock, bog and heather. And there is God to be felt, so much closer when the clutter of life has been set aside in the valley below.

I parked in a lay-by near the little village of Dundonell. The day was cloudy bright, and I was intimidated by the challenge before me. Basic preparation was important. I checked my kit carefully, gauged the weather, then set off through the wood. The path was hard to find through the mass of rhododendrons, swampy grass and bog, and my feet were soon soaked.

Not an auspicious start! To my left, a stream poured in torrents down through a rocky defile, swollen by snowmelt; on the other, the trees seemed impenetrable. But eventually I found a way through, and emerged on to a hillside of heather and rock, and the occasional tree.

In the middle distance lay the rim of snow-capped mountains crowned by An Tealloch. As I threaded my way upward they looked more and more forbidding. The going was tough, and I wrestled with my insecurities. The barren landscape had no signs of life at all: no bird in the sky, no animal, not even the buzz of an insect.

Not that I felt *alone*: there was a strong sense of Presence. Here lay a paradox. Within me lay a strong assurance of God, my protector and guide. Before me lay God in his mountain fastness, stern and forbidding. Could I make it there and back before darkness fell? Could I get back in one piece? The quiet voice within said: 'Don't get this out of proportion. Keep going: all will be well.'

Encouraged, I worked my way up through the glacier valley. At last I stopped by the rim of the cwm under the snow-capped rocks. This was far enough. I listened to the silence. A faint breeze rippled the surface of the water. I felt a sort of reverence mingled with fear.

I had something to eat and drink, thinking of Moses and the elders of Israel on Mount Sinai. I was alone with my God, open to a dark grandeur and a power that – to say the least – was awe-inspiring, but at the same time transforming. It was good to be there, and as I beat a retreat down to the green valley below I knew I had been 'marked'.

Of course, God is far beyond anything I can understand, even with the help of Gerard Manley Hopkins or the metaphysical poets, but here for the first time in that rim of mountains I had encountered a God who is neither cosy nor comfortable. The paradox I now live with is the strong assurance of the God within, and the dawning discovery of a God who, in the words of the psalmist, 'breaks the cedar trees . . . splits the flames of fire [and] shakes the wilderness of Kadesh'.

It *would* be terrifying. In fact, it's immensely exciting! If it won't be noted in my logbook as a great mountain walk, this passion in my lifeblood had led me to this place and this awakening. Mountain walks won't be the same. I am grateful.

Paul Cressall

Birdwatching

I have been a birdwatcher since my days in primary school, having been introduced to the hobby through the *Observer's Book of Birds*, which was published by Frederick Warne & Co. at a cost of five shillings. At its peak in the 1960s, the book sold 1,040,400 copies.

You can watch birds virtually anywhere, of course, from your own back garden to the rugged splendour of the West Highlands of Scotland and the expansive plains of Africa. In a sense, that is a parable for seeking God – you can do it on your 'local patch', amid the familiar, or travel to a special place (a retreat centre?) and even abroad (pilgrimage site?) if your finances and ambition allow for it.

Above all, birdwatching demands patience. I have found that birds will not appear to order even in a well-known habitat, and in the words of Robert Lynd: 'In order to see birds it is necessary to become part of the silence.' Patience and silence both apply to our efforts to discover God and the reward is a certain serenity (the product of sitting quietly and focusing on nature) and an at-one-ment with creation (through engaging with the Creator God).

The sheer beauty and grace of some species, the kingfisher and avocet to name but two, take one into another dimension . . . what we would currently call the 'wow factor', bordering on a spiritual experience. But one must not forget 'the little brown jobs' – the sparrows, for example, birds the Bible describes as being 'sold at five for two pennies'. They may not be exotic but not one sparrow is forgotten by God. In other words, you do not have to be flash to be valued.

In some places you would now be hard-pressed to find five sparrows. Historically, birds, or the lack of them, have been an indicator of things going wrong in our care of the environment – God's world – which, when it was established, was described as 'very good'. This year people are talking about the absence of the cuckoo whose call is one of the easiest of bird songs to recognize. If we continue to abuse God's world and use it selfishly and unsustainably, then how many more birds will have to vanish before we wake up to our marginalization of God and his provision of 'all good gifts around us'?

Bill Page

Dogs

As a timid child I found plenty in the world to be afraid of – the dark, strangers, new situations, 'rough' sports and games, frightening films on television . . .

One thing that stands out by its absence from this long list is dogs. I have hardly ever had occasion to be afraid of dogs. Instinctively I recognized them as fellow creatures and potential allies.

My childhood reading was littered with wonderful fictional dogs. The Famous Five had Timmy, William had his faithful hound Jumble, and in some tales dogs featured as the chief characters – Blackfriars Bobby, and Prince Llewellyn's dog Gellert whose story of misinterpreted loyalty and bravery is told on a stone tablet near his grave at Bedgellert in Snowdonia – a place of pilgrimage for me.

Dogs feature large in literature – which neatly combines another of my passions. Not just the imagined ghastly Hound of the

Baskervilles and Jack London's heroic White Fang but real canines such as Elizabeth Barrett Browning's lapdog Flush; and John Steinbeck's travelling companion Charley the standard poodle. Then there are James Thurber's touching and funny stories about his various dogs and the joy that they gave. Recently there has also been John Grogan's compelling account of life with Marley, 'the world's worst dog'.

Literary insights into the dog's life and mind have been fleshed out by my contact with real-life canines. As the conditions never seemed to be right for me to have my own dog, I have lived out my passion vicariously by looking after other people's.

When I have care of a dog, life seems to have an added dimension. I feel better physically (that's because of the walking) and more cheerful (that's because of the tail-wagging every time I come into the room). Having a living, sentient being to look after is an excellent way to get 'taken out of' oneself.

Among the many admirable qualities they exhibit, dogs are: affable, fearless, devoted, enthusiastic, straightforward and optimistic (especially about walks and the possibility of food!). Most of all, they give those who are good to them unconditional allegiance.

To me, these are the same as many of the qualities that inform the spiritual life and the quest for God. When caring for a dog, I become aware of myself as a valued, special person – which I take to be the assumption at the heart of faith.

I feel more focused in the present moment and the practical task of caring helps to calm my anxieties about many things beyond my control. I find the dog's uncomplicated joy in the natural world infectious and become more appreciative of its beauty – not least because I actually take time to look at some of it.

From the dog's positive attitude I can learn key lessons about living: to trust my own enthusiasms and instincts about what is good, to value the ever-changing, ever-passing pattern of life's joys and hopes, and most of all to be courageous and hopeful in the face of the promise held out by each new day.

Michael Rowberry

Working out

I remember a grey November evening some years ago, when I was working at Bradford University, playing football for the Peace Studies Dept against Chemical Engineering. The ball came to me on the corner of the penalty area. I pushed it to the side of the defender, looked up, saw the keeper off his line and chipped it. Time stood still, a moment when you just knew everything was right, there was a felt harmony, a oneness with the ball, the turf, even the breeze, and it sailed into the top corner. Have you ever had that experience? That sense of unity with what is around you, interrelatedness, a feeling of touching a profound connectedness? Another example from the beautiful game: I remember Eric Cantona, the famous Manchester United midfielder from the mid 1990s, describing what was for him a positively spiritual moment, watching the perfection of a pass from Pelé to Carlos Alberto in the 1970 World Cup final, where Alberto did not have to break his stride as he swept in Brazil's fourth goal. Its timing, its coordination, its pure fit to the physical circumstances took Cantona's breath away. And this harmony, this sense of connectedness, can be felt not just with the world around us but at times between people too. Mark Dowd, a former monk, made a Channel Four film on football and religion, and managed to get a ticket for the European Cup final between Manchester United and Bayern Munich in 1999. Towards the end of that amazing game he realized that everybody he loved in the world was watching that one small ball. Here for him there was a deep experience of connectedness across continents and generations.

It seems to me that there are times in our lives when we experience a unity, a connectedness and a beautiful harmony that speaks to our souls deeply. Maybe it's part of being human to experience moments of true perception about those things that touch you so intimately that you suddenly really see. And what's seen, read or heard at such a moment has such a ring of truth about it that you know it's the real deal.

For me that happens most frequently through going to the gym. I've been going for 27 years, mainly running on the treadmill, a bit of arm and stomach work, and more and more yoga in recent times. It is a time of reconnection with my body and of being earthed in the reality of my immediate environment – having a job that is sedentary and largely cerebral it's all too easy to become disconnected, and it brings me back to myself and gives a healthy sense of perspective on my work and its immediate challenges, as well as giving me energy and an endorphin rush!

But actually, it's deeper than that; it's deeper than reconnection too. The late John O'Donohue wrote in his book *Divine Beauty* of how the possibilities that are open to us are deeper than just connectedness. There's the possibility of *communion* if we take time, find the space and have the patience and gentleness to enter that embrace; speaking of beauty, he writes: 'When the heart becomes attuned to her restrained glimmerings, it learns to recognize her intimations more frequently in places it would never have lingered before.' I find that the physical exercise of the gym attunes me in ways I'm frequently surprised at, and it makes me more alert to what O'Donohue calls Beauty and Presence. It doesn't just bring me back to myself but takes me into something more.

Having the time to reflect on this on the treadmill(!), I'm reminded of those words in the New Testament about how 'in [Jesus] all things were created . . . created through him and for him . . . in him all the fullness of God was pleased to dwell, and through him to reconcile to himself all things' (Colossians 1.16–20, RSV). This suggests it's Jesus' signature that is there, on creation, his beautiful trace, his presence shot through creation. The experiences I've just described, about a sense of connectedness and unity – these experiences tie in for me to this sense of Jesus as the One in whom 'all things hold together'. But even more than this, that same passage suggests to me that Jesus is the goal of creation. For me those experiences of communion, those fleeting glimpses of beauty, might just be foretastes of that sense of coming home, that dazzling splendour, that waits for us, in him.

And I guess for me it begins to tie up with other experiences. Like being alone on a star-lit night, hearing a pebble drop in a quiet pond with a solitary splash, feeling my child's hand in mine, and I'm *there*. It's a hint of connectedness with it all: glimpsing, if only fleetingly, that underneath my anxieties, insecurities and fears is a beauty and a love for communion, a hint of a homecoming to beat all homecomings.

Mike Harrison

Swimming

It was about ten years ago that I decided to take up swimming, partly for my health and partly for my spiritual well-being. I had become self-employed having taken early retirement from my university. I found this gave me more flexibility but also some challenges in the way I structured my life. These came together when my doctor suggested I take up swimming as an exercise and I also felt this might be a way of setting aside time for prayer while I swam. Certainly other ways of setting aside time that I tried had not worked.

I started to swim three times a week and tried praying while I swam. It was hopeless; before I was halfway down the first length my mind had wandered on to all the other things in my life. I then thought more about prayer and decided that although I could not offer prayer with words I could make the time set aside as prayer in itself, irrespective of what my thoughts were . . . It is, I suppose, a sort of silent meditation. I remembered hearing a nun talk about the boredom of going through the same prayers every day for years and saying that her prayer was 'giving that time to God'. I did the same as an act of faith and it has now become part of my 'Rule of Life'. It provides me with a spiritual 'break' to allow my overactive brain to stop occasionally and let God into my life.

A while afterwards I resolved to make my swimming structure more 'robust' by buying a season ticket. It worked! It gets me through the winter and the days when I don't want to go. I was tripped up for a while by starting to time myself to see if I could improve my speed, and then found if I did a slow time I would feel disappointed and that could spoil the whole experience. It was meant to be relaxing! I had slipped back into a competitive and goal-oriented mode which I was trying to move away from. I stopped timing and sometimes now make a conscious effort to swim really slowly and enjoy the experience of being in the water.

Much of the time the experience is very ordinary. I just go, swim, and come home. I don't think I pray any more in the conventional sense but it does help me to stop thinking and try to tune in to a more intuitive approach to life. I usually get a better sense of perspective after I have swum, and just occasionally I find that I 'lose myself' in the water. It is what might be described as a 'Zen' type moment of oneness, what sportspeople and musicians describe sometimes as being 'in the zone'. Unfortunately for me it doesn't mean swimming any better but it does give a simple moment of enjoyment, a feeling of 'at-oneness' with the water. This in itself seems to be a sort of prayer.

Swimming most days gives a valuable balance to my life and makes an important contribution to establishing a spiritual 'anchor' in my day. With a few other things it has given me a robust structure that helps me with the slippery process of prayer.

RG

Dancing

Catapult, basket, wurlitzer, flat spin push, ballroom drop . . . just five of the many dance moves I enjoy when dancing Ceroc, a cross between rock and roll and jive. With a confident partner I can be spun, dropped, turned, even thrown up in the air and caught again – it's totally exhilarating.

On top of that, there's the pulse and throb of the dance music, the companionship of other enthusiastic dancers and the satisfaction and stimulation of learning new and ever more complex sequences. Sometimes the pace is gentle and slow, at other times fast and frenetic with acrobatic and dramatic moves. There are an estimated 500 moves to learn!

When I'm in the middle of spinning round and round I can feel pure joy welling up inside me. I feel so fully alive and very conscious of how blessed I am to have the health and strength to dance. Sometimes as I spin and twirl in synchronization to music and partner there are moments when I remember the words of

Eric Liddell, the Olympic gold medal runner: 'When I run I feel his pleasure.' Dare I say that when I dance I feel his pleasure? I sense God saying, 'I enjoy seeing you happy, I enjoy seeing you express yourself, I am a generous, lavish, extravagant God who delights in creativity and energy and vibrancy.'

Sometimes I can feel that same sense of joy just observing others dancing together in harmony. It helps me reflect that I can find contentment in watching and being, and not just in doing.

Some couples have their own conspicuously unique style, which reminds me that in the sight of God I too am an original! I need to hear that often as I struggle with feeling insignificant in a busy hierarchical and complex world.

I have to admit that I don't enjoy every dance. Some partners, especially those who are raw beginners, have little synchronization and their arm and leg movements are wooden and jerky. At times like these I am tempted to be critical and impatient with my partner. It would be easy to flounce off or be critical so the other person could easily feel a failure. But I know that this is not how God would want me to be. So dance can be an opportunity for me to pray for and learn patience.

Likewise, when life isn't the smooth dance I would like it to be, God is there challenging me to let him transform me and my negative attitudes.

I've never had a problem linking God and dance together. They've been a natural combination since my early twenties, when jigging about at a disco I first heard an authoritative, calm, inner voice that I believe was God speaking to me.

Thirty years later, both on the dance floor and in life I am very much 'work in progress'. I still have much to learn and many more new Ceroc moves to master.

Sue Shaw

The Stones

I can remember buying the first Rolling Stones LP, and carrying it home feeling proud and excited. They were the band that I loved to listen and dance to as a young man. There was a group of us who used to gather on a Saturday night in one another's homes to party. The lads would probably have played football together in the morning, and most of us would have cycled across the Lea Valley to watch Spurs in the afternoon, and then in the evening the girls would join us and we'd drink and dance the night away. At least that's how I remember it! Music, football and girls: the stuff of this young man's dreams.

When we'd had a few beers we did what we thought was quite a passable imitation of the Stones, leaping and strutting about, playing our instruments. It was the hard driving beat, the frenetic energy and the irreverent attitude to all things establishment, that spoke to us. And the exuberant sense of feeling so alive as we danced. I wouldn't have made the connection between those things and God then, but I can see it now.

And it's never gone away. I can recall hearing 'Satisfaction' for the first time on a transistor radio while doing Voluntary Service Overseas in the Pacific, between school and university. It came from a radio station in Townsville, Australia and it sounded fantastic.

I remember the deep satisfaction at ending a sabbatical period a couple of years ago by going to a Stones concert with a mate. It was a huge crowd, a warm night, and a magnificent display of lights, theatre and throbbing music, orchestrated by this small group of elderly gentlemen whose fitness levels defied belief. And I was jumping up and down and singing like a kid again. And then just a couple of days ago I went to a friend's fiftieth birthday party. After the food was eaten and the speeches were delivered, the crowd thinned as its elderly members retired to their beds; then the music started and eventually the Stones were playing again. There I was, leaping about, surprising myself, and possibly embarrassing others, with my sprightly and deft footwork. At least that's how it seemed to me.

Where's God in all this? Well, all over the place. God's there in the pounding beat that brings my body alive, and the overwhelming sense of release in being taken out of myself in the corporate response. God's there in the exciting sense of being on the creative edge. God's there in the slightly anarchic, rude gestures to the establishment both within and without that are such a part of the band's appeal. Think early Old Testament prophets and their wild activities; think King David dancing before the Lord and embarrassing his wife; think Mary shouting out the words of the Magnificat that celebrate a God who turns everything upside down; think Jesus himself leaving home and telling his family that they were no longer his mother and his brothers. Think of the subversive God, who questions all our comfortable assumptions, who challenges us always to be explorers, who occasionally overwhelms us with the power of the Spirit. Think the Rolling Stones!

I see this picture before me. I am an old man in a seedy nursing home, slumped in my chair. One of the staff puts on some music in the hope of bringing back a memory or two and inducing a little life. It's the Stones! Slowly I drag myself up onto my zimmer, and begin to move, slowly at first but then faster and faster, until I slump and collapse to the floor, summoned by the Lord to a greater place. What a wonderful way to go.

HM

Justice

Justice, the state of the world, politics, campaigning – these are all things that 'the world' (evil, separated from God, going to hell) does. They are not for true believers who 'love the Lord'. So ran one of the narratives of my youth.

Over the years I grew out of this but it was not easy. Leaving that kind of certainty was a slow process, sometimes painful, yet joyful at the same time. Someone said to me years ago, 'God is more concerned about how we treat one another than about what we do in our bedrooms.' That has become a guiding light for my conscience.

Still justice and activism were not really for me – until a short awareness-raising visit to Israel and Palestine with Christians Aware, meeting many workers for peace and justice (Palestinians and Israelis), sent me home shocked by what I had seen. It was the nearest thing to a 'conversion experience' that I have known – an inner conviction that I must get involved. I began to participate in marches and parliamentary lobbies – yes, me!

Finally I screwed up my courage to apply to be an Ecumenical Accompanier (<www.quaker.org.uk/eappi>; <www.eappi.org>) and was accepted. I've served two three-month periods as an EA in the West Bank, observing, accompanying, learning about an incredibly complex conflict. Since then I have spoken to many varied groups, raising awareness of the situation.

And this passion for justice has moved me towards the fringes of the organized church. Justice, poverty, human rights in their best form – these are what Jesus is all about. For me 'church' simply doesn't 'do it'. I'm drawn towards the Quakers because they *are* doing it, often at great cost; perhaps that will be the next step on my journey of questioning and learning.

Patricia Price-Tomes

Novel reading

I keep novels in the workplace. In a study full of practical papers and jobs to be done there are two bookcases of fiction. They are like the wardrobe doors into Narnia.

For me there is pleasure in the mechanics of reading each novel. It begins with discovering the novel in the bookshop: perhaps it is another book by a favourite author, an intriguing title, a prize winner, or often I simply judge a book by its cover. Back at home the novel sits on the 'ready and waiting' shelf before the first page is turned. I love the anticipation. The front page is the start of a journey. Not just the first pages, but every time I open the book I am currently reading, I have a sense of travelling into a new place.

Like many people, my life is ordinary. It is spent in an obscure suburb of a northern town of little beauty and excitement. Sometimes the journey of a novel will take me to wonderful places with beautiful landscapes, fabulous homes, delicious meals or into an adventure. Novels give me an intensity of experience that cannot be felt in ordinary life. Above all, I love them because they are full of people. A novel brings me into the company of new friends: people to admire and love, others who will enrage and frustrate me, but the novel offers the opportunity to explore the minds of others.

A good story is very satisfying. It touches on a range of emotions. I can find myself laughing out loud, or spitting rage over an injustice, or encouraged by a picture of human compassion and selflessness, or feeling broken-hearted with a jilted lover. All this feels very therapeutic.

I relish the sense that the writer is in control and he or she will lead me on a safe journey, although we may go to dangerous and forbidden regions. The reader can inhabit all sorts of places that could never be available to an individual in a lifetime. Some of these situations are frightening. There is no pleasure in sitting among drug dealers or being inside a torture chamber but experiencing such dark places in a novel offers a glimpse of experience that others have really known. Far from being an escape from reality, there is the possibility in fiction of hard truth staring me in the face.

I believe that God's creation is beautiful and good but because it is flawed there is darkness too, and the novel allows me to see more of all of that, especially when the writer is observant of the minutiae of created order and the human mind. Sometimes a novelist helps me to make sense of half-formed ideas and that deepens my understanding of God's world. For me Christ's incarnation is the key to hope. In his complete participation in the world and human experience I find connection with divine life. In novels that help me to know more of the world and further explore human nature I see more of him. It is not that the great novelist captures and contains the mystery of life found only fully in divine life, but that he or she reveals more and more of it that I could not otherwise see.

The exciting thing is, there are more great novels out there than I have the time or energy to read, so the possibilities for new discoveries and thus journeys into God are endless.

Sue Bond

Sudoku

I can remember very clearly when I first discovered Sudoku. I'm not sure that I would call it an 'epiphany' but perhaps I should.

I was bored on Newcastle railway station as I waited for a connection, and was browsing in a bookshop. There on a shelf was a book of puzzles of which I'd heard but to which I'd paid no attention before. I took a chance, bought a copy, and within minutes I was hooked!

A Sudoku is a number puzzle. It consists of a large square with nine small squares along the top and nine down the side: a total of 81 squares. The large square is also divided into nine medium-size squares, three small squares wide and three down. Each medium square contains the numbers one to nine, as does each line, vertical and horizontal, on the large square. Some squares are filled in, to give some clues as to which numbers go where (quite a lot on easy versions of the puzzle, far fewer on the difficult ones) and you then have to work out the rest.

Sudoku has taught me many things:

1 It's a good way for me to relax after a busy day. But it is no use trying to solve one when I am tired. I need to be fresh.
2 I have to trust that there is an answer to the puzzle, which is discoverable, although I can never see it to begin with.
3 I need to proceed one step at a time. I start by completing what is obvious and easy, and then try to build on that.
4 I can proceed both positively and negatively. Sometimes I can see that a number must fit that space. Sometimes I can see that it won't go there, or there, or there, so it must go here.
5 There often seems to be a crucial clue that may be difficult to see, but once found opens up a whole section of the game, or occasionally the entire game.
6 If I get totally stuck, cheating by looking at the solution at the back of the book doesn't help much. It may show where I've gone wrong. But because there is a flow to the game, just filling in one number without knowing why may not help at all, and can be positively misleading.
7 If I am stuck, I may put it down and come back to it later. When I do, it's often surprising how what had before seemed like a muddle now seems very clear and obvious.

8 Or if I am really sick and tired of this puzzle that has defeated me, then I can erase my answers and try again, often with greater success.

9 There is often a wonderful sense of achievement on successful completion.

There seems to be much life and faith wisdom in all this.

It's good to take a chance.

It's not easy to pray or do anything important when I'm tired; I need to be fresh. Faith requires me to trust that there is meaning in my life even if I can't see it. I have to proceed one step at a time and trust that the way forward will become clear.

Sometimes I make progress by seeing things and sometimes by deducing from what I can't see.

There can be sudden flashes of insight.

Sometimes everything comes together in a wonderful and up-lifting way, and sometimes it doesn't.

The puzzle, like God, is very forgiving, and is always willing to give me a second chance.

HM

12

God in our pain

———◆•◆•◆———

Introduction

If you ask people today what it is that makes belief in a loving God difficult, most will probably reply that it is all the suffering in the world. It is an interesting question in itself as to why this should be seen to be so. But it also presents something of a paradox for Christians, who have at the centre of their faith an image of a loving God dying on a cross, in the midst of suffering.

The biblical witness, as we have seen, frequently speaks of a God who is experienced through, despite of, or in the midst of suffering and pain. When people talk with me of their faith stories it is not unusual for them to tell of a God they encountered most profoundly in their most painful times.

And that is my experience as well. The experience is still pretty vivid, although in fact it took place quite a long time ago now. It happened when my marriage fell apart, and an excruciatingly painful time it was too. I am usually someone who falls asleep in no time and who stays asleep until the morning, but I went through a long spell of waking in the night and being unable to get back to sleep, because I was worrying about all the possible consequences for all of us who were involved. Problems can seem unsolvable at four in the morning, so these were difficult times. Then one night I woke up and totally to my surprise felt myself held and addressed by God. The words spoken to me were not very original, but their power came from the sense of being personally addressed. The problems did not go away, and indeed took a long time to begin to resolve themselves, but the deep angst lifted, for I now knew that nothing could separate me from the love of God.

Remembering this, and reading the contributions that make up this chapter, a number of reflections come flooding back. I remember with gratitude the number of good people who acted as supportive friends, not taking sides, not passing judgement, but just being there as accepting friends. I also remember those who stood in judgement and told me what I must or must not do.

I remember the importance of saying a Daily Office (see pages 85–6) of prayer morning and evening, often with other people: it provided me with a framework that held me when much else in life felt in flux. I know that as I reflected on what had happened, and was still happening, I learnt, and continue to learn, much about myself. I know that my relationship with God changed gear dramatically. I had never experienced God so powerfully and personally present before, and I knew that I wanted to build my life on this new experience. I discovered a feminine face of God that I had only known previously in theory. And it changed my understanding of priesthood, renewing it in a wonderful way.

It has turned out to be a source of blessing for me. I find myself quite reluctant to write that. I guess that is partly because it was such a painful time; partly because on the face of it, it would have been so much better for all of us if we had not had to go through it; and partly because I don't know, and have little influence over whether it will prove to be a blessing to the rest of our family. I can only trust that to God, which often seems like a 'big ask'.

We would all prefer to avoid pain and suffering if we can, and we live in a society that is often too keen, in my view, to find someone else to blame when things do not go smoothly. But the reality of life seems to be that pain and suffering can't be avoided: they are a part of the given-ness of life. We need rather to find a creative way of handling them. It's not rocket science to suggest that a story of a hideously painful death followed by a resurrection might have something to teach us about this. Although we need to beware the assumption that the story provides a simple template for all possible responses to suffering. The narrative of Jesus walking away from the confrontation in Nazareth when the crowd wanted to stone him offers a very different model, for example.

It's important to remember, I think, that Jesus invites his followers to take up their own cross and follow him. He doesn't invite us to pick up someone else's cross, or to go around looking for crosses to pick up, but simply to pick up our own, which I take to mean facing and owning our individual pain and suffering. Luke has him saying that we need to do this each day.

The gospel seems to suggest that if we face and own our pain, then it will, in its particular time and way, lead us to a resurrection of sorts. Facing and owning our pain doesn't necessarily mean meekly accepting it. It might mean challenging and confronting it. But however we handle it, facing and owning our pain will become a source of blessing: it will lead to a new, deeper and richer sense of life. The Gospel doesn't promise that the way will be easy (it will frequently be very painful), or in our own control (which is even more difficult), and it doesn't offer any guarantees (which is scary indeed). It doesn't suggest that there won't be lessons we need to learn along the way. But it does suggest that there is meaning to be found in it, however unlikely that may often seem.

If facing our own pain and suffering can be a path to God then it's not a path that is exclusively trodden by those of the Christian faith. Everybody walks this path in one way or another at some time in their life, and they may well encounter a God of love on their journey whether or not they are carrying a Christian membership card. Many of them will respond to that God, named or unnamed. Many will find themselves ministering to us, as some of our contributors suggest, perhaps being experienced by us as angels: messengers of the loving God. This loving God who seeks us out seems to do so under many guises, most of which we don't notice, perhaps because we have deep prejudices as to how, and through whom, God can meet us. Perhaps we have deep prejudices as to what sort of God we are in fact dealing with here. Maybe, just maybe, part of the point of the pain and the suffering is to break down some of those prejudices?

We clearly cannot cover all of life's painful situations in this chapter. Some of those here you may know from personal experience, but you may reflect differently on them; others may be new to you. We are not suggesting that these reflections offer *the* way to reflect on these things, or that each writer has said all that they might wish to say, but they offer *a* way.

Hopefully they will offer ways that stimulate deeper and renewed reflection on your own experience. You might like to write something for your own personal benefit. And if you'd like to send it by email to Roy and myself (see <www.annunciationtrust.org.uk/>) we'll be pleased to consider adding it to the Annunciation Trust website for others to read and perhaps be inspired by.

HM

Losing Iona

News of a fourth child on the way was a surprise, and as we got used to the idea, an exciting prospect. The church was pleased that the vicarage would have a baby in residence. The older, almost teenage, children looked forward to the change. Part-way during the pregnancy we were told that there was a 1 in 120 chance that there would be a problem, but that if it were so the child would almost certainly not survive to birth. The day came and little Iona was born. She had Edwards' syndrome, a chromosome abnormality similar to Down's syndrome. We were offered the opportunity to take her home to die and we grabbed the chance. We expected her to live a few days at most but she shared her life with us for almost 18 months. Initial anger and grief turned to gratitude for having her with us. Characteristic of Edwards' syndrome are pixie-like features and very slow growth. Iona remained a tiny baby for the whole of her life. She was small and sweet enough for any person, old or young, to enjoy a cuddle. At the end of Sunday services we had to search for her as during the morning she was passed from person to person, all eager for their turn!

The emotions I felt around her birth were aimed at God. I knew that God wasn't 'to blame'. But I still needed to shout at him and express what was going on inside. While holding intellectual acknowledgement that I am not immune to the usual pressures of humankind I could not apply that to the way I felt. My head and my heart went in opposite directions. In retrospect I can see that treating God unfairly enabled me to support my family and others in the community who were deeply shocked. I know that I was using God as a scapegoat. I don't feel guilty about it – that is the business he is in. Expressing myself with vigour to God when no one else was around enabled me to express my grief and anger in a more appropriate and moderated way to others who themselves needed support. Familiar words from Isaiah 53 – 'Surely he took up our infirmities and carried our sorrows . . .' – have taken on a new significance for me. God quite uncomplaining bears whatever I can throw at him, however unjust. And in taking that he releases me to future ministry.

Having got used to Iona's presence we realized it was time to move on. Iona came with us on interview and was a big asset. Who could resist her charm? We moved into the new parish with a start date set. Five days after we moved, and before anyone in the parish had met Iona, she died. We had had a number of scares and visits to hospital in her short life. We knew we would not have her for ever. But we didn't expect it to happen like this – no warning and alone in her new bedroom. We and the new parish were looking forward to her ministry of cuddles growing in a new environment. I felt cheated. Why had God tagged us along? We didn't expect Iona to live but it seemed as though she was going to be able to make her mark in our new parish. Suddenly we were plunged into a very dark place, with our new church community unable to share our grief. They tried, of course, but they didn't know her. It felt very lonely without her. Our other children started their new schools and could not explain what they were feeling – their new friends had never met their sister. It felt as though God was being extremely cruel. Why build our hopes up only to dash them at the most vulnerable point in our lives?

Nine years on we still feel it was unfair. It just feels mean. All we can do is continue to complain. And regularly releasing our bitterness onto God enables us to go on. We would not have swapped Iona for any other child. She was very precious. Some disabled children can be very special – completely dependent and trusting. When they die the carer loses their job and their main purpose in life, as well as losing a constant companion. Rebuilding life is a difficult process. Fortunately for us we were already in the process of adopting another child (because we enjoyed Iona so much). Over the years two other children have joined our family. Without Iona's influence we would probably not have entertained the idea of adopting disabled children. Without God as scapegoat we could never have rediscovered our balance sufficiently to take on the new challenges.

Paul Tudge

An autistic child

The discovery that our third child, Mark, has severe autism, and the consequences of living with him for the last 16 years, have had a profound effect on my faith and on my approaches to prayer.

First, there was simply the coming to terms with having a child with a disability. There are the practical issues, fighting for the right educational and social provision, which is if anything more difficult now he is a teenager than it was when he was three. There is the fact that he would need care for the rest of his life, that even now we cannot let him out on his own, or leave him alone in the house.

But alongside those concerns was the need to grow through it spiritually and emotionally. The usual expectations you have for a child are turned on their head; the pattern of dependent baby and toddler gradually growing in independence and of a growing, maturing relationship between parent and child is halted in its tracks. Spiritually, even though I did not find myself asking the question, 'Why me?' – I came to know too many more in worse situations than we were – as a minister in the church we found other people were trying to answer the question for us. 'It's all for a purpose,' they said, or, 'Let me come and pray for healing for him so that God's glory will be revealed.' These responses we found very difficult to cope with.

Autism is sometimes helpfully described as a condition with a triad of impairment: social interaction (relationship), social communication and social imagination. Mark is significantly impaired in all these three areas, and I came to realize that these were the three areas that inspired my spirituality and prayer life. I see faith, and particularly prayer, in terms of a relationship with God, sustained by communication and imagination. Where did Mark fit into the picture?

I have to say that answering that question is still an ongoing process. There are no easy answers.

From the start I have known that from my experience of God, Mark must be very special to God. A God who cares for the outsider and welcomes all cannot reject one like Mark, even if Mark can never form a 'relationship with God' in ways that make sense to me.

I have learnt that many people, particularly men, have elements of autism in their personality, and so am on a journey in growing in appreciation that the way that God becomes real to me in my prayers, through relationship, communication and imagination, cannot be the only way. I have learnt to respect more formal, less feeling-based expressions of faith, even if they don't speak to me.

For me the story has no 'happy ending', no triumph over suffering. There are still times when the weight of Mark's presence in the home seems to drive out the things that are precious to me in my faith. My own prayer life has had to become more formal and less spontaneous to prevent it becoming squeezed out.

The question, 'Where is God in this?' has no clear answer, but I know that exploring the question is continuing to give me profound insights into the nature of the human condition and enlarging my understanding of God, in ways that would have been impossible without Mark, and for that, sometimes, I give thanks.

One of the most difficult things about autistic people like Mark is that they don't reciprocate expressions of love in ways that others do. There is usually no payback. So when people go out of their way to care for Mark it is an expression of grace. The young people who assist in the play schemes Mark goes to in the holidays are wonderful examples of this, in the care they take to ensure Mark has a good time, even though he can give no clear indication of whether he is really enjoying himself or not.

I saw it at first hand a couple of years ago when I was in the supermarket queue with Mark. The shop had lifts just by the checkout. Mark kept running off to play in the lift and as I followed him I kept losing my place in the queue. Eventually I got hold of him and hugged him tight to stop him running off, only for him to start screaming the place down. I was contemplating abandoning the shopping completely when a teenage girl, whom I didn't know, came up to me and said: 'I'll have Mark if you want. I know him from the play scheme.' And she took him off for a few minutes, and I was able to pay for my shopping. It was an act of grace that I shall never forget, and surely a parable of the grace of God, not just for Mark, but for all.

Ian Howarth

Blindness

I was able-bodied and very healthy until I was involved in an accident in August 2005. Now I am visually limited. Still I can say that my way after the accident is coloured by the love of the Holy One.

After a serious accident I woke blind in an intensive care ward in a hospital in Windhoek (Namibia). I couldn't talk because of a canule, a tube in my throat, my arms were securely fastened and I felt pain in my face. My first thought was: 'Let me die.'

But very soon I realized: my wife is alive, I love my children and grandchildren, people saved my life. I want to live, I can live. I will trust in the outcome of this process, I will be loved by the Holy One. It will be possible to live as a beloved child of God.

That was not a thought, but a knowing within my heart. A present, a gift of the Holy One. I didn't fight for this. For me it was a way of accepting, beginning with this unknown journey. For others it might be important to give attention to your anger or despair. I felt the love of the Holy One in the attentive help of doctors and nurses, in the intensive prayers of so many people around us. Receiving was an important task of life for me in this period.

Now I have the limited sight of one eye only.

I learnt the wisdom of the deeper meaning of comfort. That happened first of all when I was listening to a hymn by William Cowper which begins:

Sometimes a light surprises
The Christian while he sings.

Singing this song I felt allied with so many people who suffer. It was as if they said to me: 'You are not alone on this journey.' Now I can cry and laugh. I learnt with my heart what Hildegard of Bingen said: 'our wounds can be transformed into pearls'.

I am not glad with the consequences of the accident. But still I can say that I received in it something very precious. God is more close to me and trustworthy on a deeper level. For me this is like the words of Psalm 66.10 (NRSV):

For you, O God, have proved us;
you have tried us as silver is tried.

I am for God as precious metal. He exposed my strength. The love of my wife and children has now a golden rim. My life is more intensive.

I received a letter from a colleague. She asked me carefully: 'Can you love your damaged, your disfigured face?' So I felt invited to do *lectio divina* of my body, which you can find on pages 93–4.

Gideon van Dam

Employment, redundancy and job hunting

Like most Christians, I don't find prayer easy. Whether because of not making the time, finding the time, or through having a wandering mind when I finally do get down to it, prayer does not play the part in my life that I might wish it did. But looking back, there have been times of learning and growing through prayer. In particular, a couple of instances come to mind in relation to my career and professional life.

A couple of years ago, I was going through a stressful time in my then job, working on multi-million-pound bids. An unfamiliar environment, a pressurized schedule, the threat of being sidelined, and some difficult people to work with were combining to make me feel quite depressed and inward-looking. My praying at that time was for some sort of change. To use a word that can often be associated with prayer aspirations, I was seeking a 'breakthrough'.

One day, when praying and going through a litany of complaints, and seeking some kind of breakthrough, I had a real sense of a gentle but penetrating divine rebuke. What I felt God was saying to me was that if I only associated him with a 'breakthrough', then I was denying his presence with me in the pain and difficulties. From then on I felt my attitude changed somewhat, particularly in the way I related to other people, as I focused more on God's presence with me in the present, rather than what he might do for me in the future.

Earlier this year I was made redundant and had a short period out of work. In the end, I only had five weeks between jobs, but over several months (both anticipating and following the redundancy notice) I had a prolonged period of uncertainty as regards my future work. In applying for various positions I was having quite a high success rate in securing job interviews (so at least the CV must have looked OK!) but a series of outcomes in which the disappointment of rejection was mixed with a feeling of 'Well, perhaps that wasn't for me anyway.'

Then one day I went for an interview for a contract position with a government department. Coming home afterwards I went through the usual post-mortem exercise in my mind of analysing the interview, and thinking of things I wished I had said or hadn't said and so on. Mixed in was a feeling that the job did actually sound quite interesting and challenging, so my mind was a bit of a whirlwind when I returned back to my empty house.

In the quietness I sat down and prayed. I prayed that after all the various disappointments and uncertainties, I might have a breakthrough. Unlike on the previous occasion, this time it felt right to be praying for a breakthrough and a sense of expectancy rose in me as I did so.

Needless to say I got the job and it has been both interesting and challenging. The position is not a permanent one, and my future still has its uncertainties. But for the moment, I do have that sense of being where I feel I am 'meant to be', and I guess one thing these prayer experiences has taught me is to live more in the moment, whatever our hopes or fears are for the future.

Gavin

Learning to surrender

A spider's web, bejewelled by the morning dew and illuminated by the early sunshine, offers me a snapshot of the pattern of life – for in structure and fragility it seems in various ways to resemble it. Life, like a cobweb, is finely spun and transient, exquisitely and uniquely woven with its connecting threads with many unfilled spaces in between. On dull days it may be almost unnoticeable. It provides a home for a living creature at its centre.

A shaft of sunlight occasionally illuminates it and it becomes a thing of great beauty and wholeness; it is noticed and wondered at. For all its apparent fragility the strength of the web lies in its intricate connectedness.

Looking back over what must be now a nearly completed journey, I see patterns of connectedness, sometimes broken and reconnected in new ways, but making its way towards completion.

When the spider's work is thwarted by some broken threads, she accepts the interruption and while seeming to mark time, she reinforces the place, and adapts her pattern . . . affecting the eventual shape and size of the web.

As a child I loved fairy stories, and children's versions of ancient myths, all of which fascinated me. Both of these worlds were seedbeds for imagination, but also gave me a curious sense of having come from a life I could not quite remember but to which I felt deeply connected. It gave me a sense too of being part of something both before and beyond the world I was now connecting with; I would call it spiritual awareness. I don't think that awareness has ever been absent since it is, if you like, one of the supporting radial struts of my web of my life. Now I think it finds expression in my search for God.

From time to time, unsought and apparently randomly, this same sense of connectedness is heightened; little epiphanies come sometimes through glimpses of nature, experiences in relationships, a poem or a picture, a haunting phrase of music, a dream . . .

A major moment of disconnection came at a moment in midlife when I was quite seriously ill with a bowel obstruction some while after cancer surgery and radiotherapy.

Physically and psychologically I was in a very low state and beyond knowing why the surgeons were so slow in deciding to operate. I was moved to a side ward and began the process of dying (or so it seemed at the time). I remember a very gentle and unfussy auxiliary nurse coming to wash me. It was a moment when I realized that I was totally helpless; no one had touched me and handled my body in such a gentle and loving way since I was a baby.

For someone who liked to be self-sufficient and in control it was a make or break moment. With no strength to resist such intimacy I surrendered, and the surrender was more than just a physical experience.

In doing so all my anxieties about who would finish my unfinished tasks, who would take care of people I cared for, fell away and I knew that I could confidently leave all those fears and anxieties behind, that 'nothing (that I was fretting about) mattered'. And in that moment I think the creative spider began her reparative work.

I do not know enough about spiders to know whether, in fact, they make the first supporting thread continuous with the last, so that the same thread that holds the top of the web also holds the bottom. It was that experience of contact with the final thread that connected it to the initial moment of my early memory and imprinted the experience there for ever.

It was as though, at that moment, life was gathered up, my baggage could be safely left and I could move freely towards whatever lay ahead with complete confidence and trust.

With Julian of Norwich, I knew at a profound level that 'All manner of things shall be well.'

Gill Russell

'It's all good stuff!'

I can remember it as if it were just yesterday! In fact it was well over ten years ago – 10 March 1997 – and I was just wondering how I would celebrate 25 rich and rewarding years in the public ordained ministry. Then the exhaustion of it all hit me. It was like an internal elastic band snapping, and with it a flood of emotion, but also the great sense of relief that I did not have to pretend any more. Why is it that we think that hiding our vulnerability is an essential part of being a priest? The weeks and months that followed were to reveal that this breakdown was in fact to be a breakthrough, an initiation into a new understanding of myself and my vocation. Looking back it is always a temptation to spiritualize such an experience, but although extremely painful this was to prove to be for me a truly God-given and God-filled time. So how did I emerge from this dark abyss and discover once more that life and ministry were not only possible but could be enjoyed?

First, I was blessed with patient, sensitive and caring companions on this demanding part of my journey. Just weeks earlier I had arranged to begin weekly sessions with a Jungian therapist and also after some searching had found a new spiritual director. After the 'crash' I was also led to a caring community in Devon, the Society of Mary and Martha. Alongside a loving and understanding wife they all provided the support I sorely needed. This sort of companionship or soul friendship is for me at the heart of the Christian experience. Jesus began his ministry by gathering a small group around him with whom he shared deeply. The life of discipleship is personal but not private. It is not about independence but an interdependence based on a common search for and trust in our God. We need each other on the journey.

Second, I was to learn the meaning of 'patiently waiting on God'. For 25 years I had thought that Christian commitment only issued in constant activity and availability. The more you cared the more you did. The language of sacrifice (which is to be found everywhere in church life) was at the forefront of my understanding. As the days lengthened and spring gave way to summer so a gentle growth and healing took place in me; but I wanted to speed it up . . . to fast forward the process . . . 'I will be better by Easter,' I told myself, only to endure a Holy Week and Easter that was a *via dolorosa* but with no resurrection. Weeks later, in June, I was to receive something of a gift of new life . . . an Easter encounter but in God's time. So I was truly to learn the essence of waiting on God and finding meaning within it.

Third, I was enabled through it all to get in touch with my own humanity, which I had nobly denied for so long, and in the midst of it discover the God made known to us in the flesh of Jesus. Surely the distinctiveness of our religion of the incarnation of God is just this: that in embracing our humanity fully rather than denying it do we discover the self-made in the image of God.

In the years of parish ministry that have followed and in my work as a spiritual director my time in the wilderness that felt at first debilitating and paralysing has proved to be an enabling and enriching experience. And as for my own inner journey? This time, rather than pointing to the absence of God, has for me renewed a sense of God's presence in the midst of it all. The words of my spiritual director, which enraged and infuriated me at the time, have turned out to be so true: 'It's all good stuff!'

Colin Travers

Divorce

If marriage is the building of a trusting and loving relationship between two people, divorce is the explosive demolition of that relationship.

I hate divorce! It hurts as much as do the jagged shards of broken glass when a fist is punched through a window.

Divorce isn't a legal process – that simply 'tidies up the paper-work'. Divorce is the breaking asunder of a marriage.

It can happen gradually, through abusive or aggressive behaviour, or through neglect. Or it can happen suddenly: a surprise to one partner, or so it would seem, caused often by an affair by the other partner. A secret shifting of the points from one track to another so that the two who were one begin, perhaps imperceptibly at first, to become two travelling separately, with the tracks ever widening from each other.

For me it was sudden – or so it seemed. Yet with almost immediate hindsight I saw chinks, and even gaping holes, that I had been aware of but had chosen not to see or accept. That showed me how honest God wants me to be with reality, however much that hurts or costs me.

I've never known anything hurt so much, or so deeply. Nor could I have imagined the extent of the atomic fallout on so many people. Divorce is hell.

What hurt the most? The betrayal. It was even sealed with a kiss – a warmer than usual kiss – as I went off to work on the morning of the Day of Destruction. Funny the things you remember when you look back. I remember thinking, 'God, I don't want to grow old alone.' And I remember a sense of God in that even though this was not an ending I wanted, there was somewhere hidden in the pain the hint of a seed of a new and even exciting beginning.

God has taught me about trust. Trust is a bit like a delicate bone-china teacup that when carelessly dropped and broken into fragments can never be properly restored. The joins and breaks are always visible, even with the best superglue and most skilled hands, and always vulnerable. Counselling helped me to come to terms with that fragility. Through it God showed me what it means to trust myself – so that I can engage in trusting relationships with others rather than a relationship of dependency, masquerading as trust.

I can well understand that for some people this shattering experience involves a divorce from God as well as from a marriage partner. Love is decimated; therefore the source of love is doubted, blamed and rejected.

For me, though, it was the source of love that held me through the agonizing and shocking pain of broken love. I was intensely aware of God in the support of friends, and the ability to organize a new pattern of life that enabled me to look after three children and continue to work as a parish priest. I was conscious of God in a deep, unfathomable way that inspired the strength to carry on. I can only describe it as a sense of hope wrapped in many layers of hopelessness.

But I have to say that this whole hellish dose of life experience has caused and enabled me to change and grow emotionally and spiritually in ways I could never have dreamed of. I wouldn't wish it on anyone else, nor would I want to have to go through it again – but I wouldn't have missed it for the world!

Through the pain I have found myself in God – a new confidence and trust; new opportunities, skills and possibilities. And I have been drawn to a closer place of trust and peace. A surprising consequence from a violent explosion!

Paul Booth

Escaping death

As I fell, I learnt that your life really does go through your mind. Not as a flash, as commonly imagined, but in very slow motion. In fact so slowly that I had time not only to review most of my life, past and present, but to begin a dialogue with God. More a one-way diatribe, to be honest, directed from me at God, explaining exactly what I would not accomplish if I were to die. I was livid that I was going to my death in this way, slipping on an ice sheet on the side of a mountain and then freely falling. I just went for it.

Clearly I lived. It was pointed out by the helicopter crew that most people they picked up were dead; a grim humour as they persuaded me to stop moving while being winched up. Later I read the newspapers describing the miracle escape and heard about the reports on the radio. And I received a postcard in hospital with the simple address of David, followed by a picture of a helicopter and the island Skye.

Lots will stay with me. Pain, as the knee ligaments torn off the bone couldn't be reconnected. And the associated frustrations of not being able to run marathons. I had the perfect build for it.

The strongest thing that stayed with me over the decades was the emotional energy that was released in my anger at God as I fell. And the list of things that I spoke. I didn't need to try to recall them, I could remember every word. They emerged from the core of my being, an expression of who I was and what I was about. By living, they were, I felt, a covenant between us.

I understood for the first time those in Mark's Gospel who shouted out at Jesus, putting their being into their yelling, overriding their friends' admonitions, demanding attention. In fact all those things I had been brought up not to do. This was a new kind of prayer for me.

Did my life change? It did. My then girlfriend burst into tears when first visiting me, saying that I was no longer the same person. I spent hours helping the person in the next hospital bed write words, spelling out letter by letter in order that they could send mail to their family. My frets and opinions diminished.

I have done every one of those things on my list, except one that remains a priority. At times I didn't focus on them and got distracted into all kinds of good works. Some took only a couple of years, some a decade, and one nearly three. However, the covenant was there, deep inside and ongoing and driving on irrespective of learning to walk again, having been told I never would; irrespective of making a living; irrespective of contributions to church life.

I learnt a new kind of prayer, a vibrant and valid expression of my being to God. It took a mountain to initiate it; sometimes a spiritual director has been alongside encouraging it; at other times my cry emerges unexpectedly. When it does cry out, I am always surprised afterwards that it never doubts that there is a listener waiting to hear.

David Pullinger

The death of my parents

My mum and dad died within a few months of each other when both were in their late eighties. I was with Mum when she died, and had spent the day of Dad's death with him although we arrived too late in the evening for his actual dying. I think that I closed the eyes of each of them.

Mum had always wanted her priest son to take her funeral, and if I am honest I would not have wanted anyone else to do so! The woman priest at the local church was kindness itself in allowing us to arrange the service just as we wished, and we sat in a circle in the chancel, with Mum's coffin in the midst of us. I wept as I led her coffin in, and my voice became fainter and fainter as we processed up the aisle. Dad, ever the Quaker, said afterwards that there were too many words.

But he later told me that he'd like me to take his service in a similar way and so I did, and again I wept and temporarily lost my voice. My brother and I laughed when they played the wrong piece of recorded music during the service, as our dad would have done had he been there.

In the weeks and months afterwards I spent time in my study in the dark with a lit candle, smoking my pipe and reflecting on it all. I needed time to process what I felt, and was surprised by the wisdom that surfaced from deep within me, and from God.

I found myself talking to my mum and using her Christian name, which I had never done before. I realized that I no longer thought of her as an old lady, that her death had somehow released me to know a more complete person. She was now a woman to me, a sister almost rather than a mother: a process aided by my aunt giving me some old family photos I had never seen before, which showed my mum as a little girl and as a young woman.

My dad had been the quiet, thoughtful, undemonstrative one who rarely expressed emotions or talked about himself. I always experienced him as being solidly supportive and accepting, but yearned for something emotionally closer. As I reflected on his life and death I slowly came to accept him as he was, not as I wanted him to be, and came to let him love me in the ways he could, and to accept that that was good enough.

My brother remarked that with their deaths we were both orphans now, and of course that's right. What I had not expected was to feel such a sense of freedom and release in the weeks that followed. Not that I had ever felt them to be oppressive parents, quite the reverse. Nevertheless their deaths felt, in a sense, like their final gift to me, setting me free in a way that surprises me.

Over the years I have spent quite a lot of time thinking about death, and have come to the conclusion that it doesn't seem to me to make much sense to assume that at death I will suddenly find myself either in heaven or in hell. I can't see why death should bring about such a sudden resolution. It seems much more likely that on dying I will still be aware that I have a lot of growing to do, to achieve peace or fulfilment or union with God, or however you want to describe it. And I find it hard to see how I will find that peace knowing that there are still people alive on earth whose lives

I have affected for ill. I will want to pray that they are able to redeem those injuries I had done them, both for their own sake and more selfishly for mine too, so that I can find peace. So my destiny is intimately bound up with all those whom I have known: salvation is a corporate as well as an individual matter.

So I now think of Mum and Dad, and indeed their parents and grandparents and generations going back to who knows when, behind them, praying for my brother and me and our families as we try to deal with issues, some of which they will have bequeathed us. Philip Larkin memorably and succinctly wrote of how our parents have a detrimental affect on us, and indeed they do, and I as a parent screw my children up too. How can it be otherwise? Indeed to a degree it appears to be necessary and good, for without a bit of grit in the system (to switch metaphors) how am I, or any of us, going to grow?

So through the deaths of Mum and Dad I see that God has given me two gifts. A deeper sense of freedom: freedom to be myself and the man God has created me to be, and therefore closer to God; and a deeper sense of my interconnectedness with all of humanity, of all God's children. By their deaths I am richer. Not what I had expected!

HM

Living with cancer

Cancer cast its shadow over my childhood: my grandfather died of cancer when I was five and my dad died of it when I was 11. My mum also died of cancer when my children were very young. So there was a sense in which I lived with cancer long before I was myself diagnosed with early stage breast cancer. I was thankful that I did not live in fear of this disease as my mother had done, but certainly the diagnosis came as a terrible shock, and in the dread and confusion I felt I was journeying in unknown territory, experiencing this horrible disease first hand.

I realize we have made great strides in the way society handles cancer. My mother had been given the news that my father had cancer by a ward sister telling her, 'It's a killer and it will kill him!'

In my case both at the hospital and with family and friends I received tremendous support and sensitive care, but there is still a sense in which you feel you are 'on your own'. I am an Anglican priest and I was used to offering comfort and support in this sort of situation, but it certainly felt very different to be on the receiving end.

I remember feeling in this new strange territory that I needed some signposts, and quite literally it was a road sign that really spoke to me at this time: 'Changed priorities ahead'. Suddenly everything felt different – I faced an operation, a course of chemotherapy and radiotherapy, and my future had a big question mark hanging over it. 'Changed priorities' gave me a marker to live by as I began to re-evaluate everything.

So where was God in all this? I felt God was very much in it all, but I experienced him not so much as the God of all comfort and strength but rather as the one who was leading me into unknown territory. This was scary and new and I felt incredibly fragile and vulnerable. But God was most definitely at the heart of it!

A Bible verse that became very important to me throughout my illness was: 'In [Christ] all things hold together' (Colossians 1.17, NRSV). There were frequent times when at one level I felt I was falling apart and nothing made sense, but at a deeper level I had a sort of assurance that it wasn't up to me to hold it together, and that in the bigger picture all would be well.

Of course, when someone experiences serious illness it is often just as hard (if not harder) for their loved ones. I had the love and support of a close family and I know it was very difficult for them.

One experience that made a deep impression on me during this time was when I was admitted to hospital with an infection. For about a week I was in a six-bed bay with five women, all of whom seemed to be much further down the road than me with terminal cancer. I found it an incredibly difficult time, and yet . . . It wasn't my health that made it difficult, it was these women, none of whom as far as I knew were regular churchgoers, showing such love, grit, kindness, humour, courage and sheer humanity. This was a huge learning curve for me. As a vicar, some might have assumed me to be a 'professional Christian', but I witnessed

Christian love in action in a way that was truly humbling. It was down-to-earth, unselfish care for one another, a kind of tough, rough and ready love in the face of their terminal illness.

It left me with big questions! Not about the existence of God – as far as I was concerned God was certainly in that bay – but rather about the foolishness of trying to contain, limit or label the work of God. It also gave me a glimpse of the God who delights to be at work in the most unlikely of places. The Big C, as cancer is sometimes known, had wreaked such havoc in the lives of those women and to some extent in my own life. But it was as though another, bigger, C had the final word – the cross of Christ, demonstrated in selfless love, was in the lives of those women and somehow had the final say!

Liz Cannon

The absence of God

I sat with my mother, as a child of about ten, making a fancy hat for a competition at the school Christmas party. The basis of our design was a circlet of plaited green material. When it was complete I said, 'It looks just like the crown of thorns.' My mother turned on me furiously and said, 'You must never make fun of Good Friday.' I hadn't been making fun, simply commenting on an obvious similarity; but the incident left me with the sense that God must always be taken very seriously.

At school we were taught stories from the Old Testament and reminded that God knew everything that we were doing. If we were naughty, even if the grown-ups didn't notice, God would see. By my mid teens I was certain that God was important and equally sure that I was a failure. God had never woken me from sleep by calling my name, or spoken to me from a burning bush. I had never seen angels descending a ladder from heaven, or received any communication at all from God as far as I could see – and it must be all my fault.

By temperament I was introverted, conscientious and questioning. I did courses, read books and married a priest (for himself, not for his dog collar), but I felt no closer to God. The sense of failure became worse because people expected the vicar's wife to know about prayer. I was quite good at playing the part, but inside was an aching, guilty emptiness made worse by the fact that I felt a hypocrite. I hated the text, 'Knock and the door will be opened to you.' I felt that I had knocked until my hands were bleeding. I never talked to anyone about the problem, I was too ashamed, and those I might have spoken to seemed dauntingly confident in their own experience of God. God knows why I didn't throw in the towel and become a happy atheist.

In my mid-thirties, while attending a quiet day, I experienced a stab of joy so deep, so intense as to be almost painful. It made no particular sense at the time, but left me exhilarated. A couple of days later on a train journey I began to remember other times when I had felt the same thing. They tended to be associated with nature, relationship or experiences of freedom, not churchy things. I began tentatively to assume that they might be related to God.

I continued to behave (and often still do) as if relationship with God is something I have to achieve by hard slog. God continues to remind me, with gentle humour, that it is not so. I took a course in Ignatian spirituality. We had to enter imaginatively into a Bible story and then talk to our small group about what had happened. The passage was the stilling of the storm. In the few spaces during a very busy week I tried without success to imagine myself in that boat on the Sea of Galilee. On the last available day I went for a country walk, found a fallen tree in the middle of a field and thought, 'Here I will be able to meditate without interruption.' I shut my eyes firmly and tried to conjure up the storm. However, the weather was not stormy at all. I was in a beautiful place with warm sunshine and a light breeze. I spoke aloud in exasperation, 'Look, God, you are not making it any easier!' For the first and only time I heard God's voice: 'Never mind that bloody boat, come and play!' So I did. Bushes don't have to be burning to be alive with God.

The absence of God was a cold, dull pain present underneath the ordinary, cheerful, busy or sad events of daily life. It was almost constant for about 15 years. It was not the same thing as depression. I have been clinically depressed. The first time was after the birth of our first child and it brought a brief interlude in the long years of distance from God. My father was dying, and I was crushed by the unexpressed grief and the responsibility of a tiny baby. We were driving by night the 200 miles to make our last visit to Dad. Suddenly I felt held by God and certain that, whatever the present difficulties, we were all safe in God's hands. Before long God was absent again, but when depression returned God came back. Perhaps it is not strange; when mind and body hit rock bottom, almost any exertion is impossible. At those times I have been forced to stop striving for God. Then there is space for God to touch me.

Mary Goldsmith

Departure from the dark God

For the past few years I had been on a mind journey into scripture. The Bible had become an exciting detective story in which its surface and literal meaning had been mined in order to find out who really had 'done' it and why. I had gone through Jesus' birth and resurrection narratives with a fine-tooth comb, teasing out what was rational and casting away what appeared to be irrational to belief in the third millennium.

I attached myself to those on a similar journey. I went to conferences and meetings where the divinity of Jesus was stripped away, but by the middle of 2007 I was the one who, strangely, felt naked. I had hammered my belief into a receptacle for containing and holding the God I had shaped into my image. Any sense of the transcendent and of encounter with the mystery had evaporated. This sense of nakedness left me feeling exposed and unprotected from the worst of myself, and my pragmatic belief left me with a God who was indifferent, dark and inexplicable. What had been grateful solitude in the company of the God-presence now became fearful loneliness created by absence.

Desert spirituality was something that had interested me for a long time. I was moved by the stories and teaching of the desert fathers and mothers, who established communities in the

Egyptian desert to which many came seeking a richer faith and encounter with God. Deep within myself I had always wanted to be in touch with their insights that centre on the heart rather than the head alone. Then, two unrelated events made possible what had really been nothing more than a vague, half-held dream. Bible-lands, through its magazine, announced a planned pilgrimage to Cairo and a four-night residential in a Coptic retreat centre in the desert. At the same time a local clergy trust fund was offer-ing substantial grants for people to explore areas of ministry and spiritual development. These two events coincided to make this dream come true, to touch the void that had opened up within my spiritual life. It was a 'coincidence' that I could not ignore.

In Cairo we visited some Coptic Orthodox churches situated in the old city. The small, simple and often ill-lit churches with their many beautiful icons and fragrance of incense began, like water running over stone, to slowly loosen my inbuilt insistence that reality is only what I had come to say it is.

Then we moved out into the desert to the Coptic retreat centre known as Anafora. The word means both to 'offer up', as when the bread and wine are offered up in the communion prayer, and to 'take off', like a bird at the moment its body lifts from the ground in flight. Our four days at this spiritual oasis in the company of the local bishop, Bishop Thomas, caused both an offering up and a taking off in my life.

The desert is a place where I met both my demons and my angels. It is in the nature of the spirituality of such a place. Like the story of Jesus in the wilderness the demons (of inner thought) came with their questioning of my faith, with their highlighting of my doubts, with their probing of my obsessions. I was, they declared, an incoherent human being on an illusory quest for fulfilment. Yet with my offering up of this acknowledgement of incoherence came the angelic-like gravitation to inner silence, reflecting the raw and penetrating silence of the desert. This inner silence spoke of the possibility of love, acceptance and belonging.

The spirituality of the desert, which imaged the desert of my heart, gave me no immediate answers, rather the realization that

I had just begun to ask the questions that could help me find my true identity and the truth that is God. What I believed to be the liberation of my mind leading up to my arrival in Egypt was simply a preparation for the beginning of the liberation of my heart, the revealing of my true identity in God.

When we left Anafora, Bishop Thomas invited us to take a piece of the desert home with us so that it might multiply in our hearts when we came back to England. I wasn't sure what that meant, but I prayed that it would be so. And it has been.

I have not returned to a purely literal understanding of scripture, nor have I sought to become an Orthodox Christian. Anafora has been built where it is because it was known that if people dug deep enough into the sand they would find flowing water. By digging deep – through prayer, reflection and contemplation, both in solitude and in the company of others – into the desert of my heart I have found the living water that Jesus spoke of to the Samaritan woman at the well in John's Gospel.

I am still learning how to be at peace because the grain of sand I returned home with is multiplying and enabling me to live with the transcendent mystery of the questions. I have learnt that, paradoxically, it is in my heart's desert I find the God from whom all life flows. And what happened to all the purely cerebral questions? They remain folded alongside the grave-clothes of an empty tomb.

Mike Catling

Caring at home

Looking back after almost seven years of post-stroke life for David, it's a good moment to reflect on how we have got through.

It has undoubtedly been a painful and frustrating time for both of us. David was living life at full tilt as a 66-year-old retired surgeon, doing counselling for different voluntary agencies. I, at a similar age, was a post-retirement curate in our local parish. Both areas of activity had to stop in the immediate impact of a major stroke.

A poem I wrote in the second year expresses the pain.

Beyond the here and now of urgent calls
That physical dependence brings
Lies a terrain of mutual sharing
Interdependence

This interlocking overlapping tethering
Hobbling of our lives together
One pair of hands and feet to meet
Two lots of bodily needs.
I screaming for respite
Yet the scream is stifled

Feeling how much worse to be
The helpless proud one
Constantly in fear of shame
Precarious shaky struggle
To survive another day
With self respect intact

God did not choose this monstrous plot
It happened
Can God recoup in us new life?
And inner freedom?

Grace, patience and practical help from family friends and professionals have helped us through. The fact that we knew many were
praying for us regularly at the beginning was an undoubted help.
Who knows how grace comes?

The prayer that I could feel made a significant difference was my
regular pattern of prayer, not only morning prayer, but evening
prayer too, around 4 p.m. before the evening shift of meal preparation and helping David into bed by 7 p.m.

That this evening may be holy, good and peaceful,
let us pray with one heart and mind.

As our evening prayer rises before you, O God,
so may your mercy come down upon us
to cleanse our hearts
and set us free to sing your praise
now and for ever.

(*Common Worship: Daily Prayer*, Evening Prayer on Sunday)

This pattern gave time to take stock of the day so far and set the compass again for grace in the evening.

Anger and frustration emerged, and most acutely in a resistance to taking part in the healing service held monthly in the parish. This service, which I had been glad to encourage at its inception, now seemed, and seems, too bland, proclaiming easy peace. And in our case no physical healing is possible. I need something grittier.

God has provided some inner freedom. For me there was acute grief in giving up a ministerial role for a retired role, just as I was getting the hang of it. There is a problem of switching from shared stroke life to ordinary life when David has times of respite care. As he says, 'We are not getting along too badly,' and we may well reach our golden wedding in three years' time. This can only be due to grace and tenacity on both our parts.

Alison Froggatt

Living with Parkinson's

I always knew I was special, but it took the consultant's diagnosis to confirm this. 'It's progressive, but you don't die of it.' Parkinson's disease had already taken up residence and I was so relieved that it was not a brain tumour that I was quite prepared to be a long-suffering martyr about whom my peers – anyone – would say, 'Doesn't he cope with it well!'

Although I'm not dealing with my demise, I have done a lot of reflecting about death and dying. I've wanted to relieve Angela of her suffering, musing on how helpful it would be for her if I was dead. At the other end of the scale, it would be a shame if my accumulated wisdom was not available finally to put the world to rights! Playing these games has kept morale high, even as, inexorably, new limitations are experienced in my body.

Angela is angry and frustrated that I am not angry and frustrated. She would expect that as a 'normal' response. But I am fairly sure that I am not into avoidance of such reactions, pushing down and bypassing them. Instead, I have a determination to confront each symptom as it appears, which means that I face up to the full implications of the changes in my body.

This can be painful as I listen to Angela express her disappointment at my loss of strength and energy and masculinity and at my slowness. Her pain includes loss of dreams of a future, and the fact that she has become a carer. She tells me of her embarrassment at being thought of as married to an old man. She even fears that new people will not know what I used to be capable of, and finds herself telling them. 'I wish they knew "the real you".' But even this does not make me angry. Instead, three of us live at home – Ned, Angela and Parkinson. The third is an unwanted guest who demands attention, imprisons us and will not leave.

I had a change of spiritual director, for geographical reasons. She has only known me since I have had PD, and so she has heard my story afresh. We have been looking at relationships. Something must have been unlocked. For . . .

I was on my own in the kitchen. Suddenly, from nowhere, I had an overwhelming sense of loss. I wept into the sink, I was racked with deep sobs and I howled. I was alone and feeling alone. I didn't want to be alone. I heard myself cry, 'I want my mummy.' I was six years old and didn't want to lose the world where I knew who looked after me.

Then, as the tearful convulsions eased, I was in a new place. Until that moment I had images of God as embracing, reassuring, nurturing. Maybe I am now discovering a God who gives me space to make my own journey. Now I can acknowledge that all those 'helpful' books and articles so kindly offered can be put to one side because God is to be found somewhere else.

Four generations of family and my beloved PD warrior Angela are not far away, reminding me that I am loved. But they can't travel with me.

I step out into my barren landscape with its distinctive sound of a wind of desolation. Here too is God. It is enough.

Ned Townshend

Remembering the fallen

The response of friends on hearing that we had been on a walking tour of the Somme battlefields felt strange, as 'Did you have a lovely time?' and 'I bet that was interesting!' came nowhere near the emotions evoked by what was really a pilgrimage to a place of horror and death for hundreds of thousands of men.

It was a beautiful area, rolling farmland punctuated by sleepy villages, similar to the Yorkshire Wolds. As on the first day of the Somme battle, the weather was perfect with wide blue skies and the odd white cloud. The fields of ripened wheat were poignantly scattered with poppies and larks were ascending and descending in full song. There was a sense of pastoral peace in the beauty of God's creation, and a difficulty in imagining the horrors of the battle that took place there almost a hundred years ago, until we reached the cemeteries.

The British soldiers were buried at the site of the battles in which they fell and the cemeteries varied in size, but each one felt overwhelming and many of our group were tearful. These young men had embarked on an exciting adventure, many having never left their villages or towns before, but their adventure included unspeakable horrors in unbearable conditions. Walking from one neat regimented stone to another evoked so many emotions. A deep sense of sadness for the loss of their future adulthood and guilt when I found that in scanning the graves, my eyes had missed a name without noting and somehow acknowledging that young man. The huge waste of life seemed to raise doubts about life's meaning and purpose, and an angry question: How could God have allowed this mass slaughter to happen?

The grief of those who had loved them was seen in the epitaphs on the graves of the men whose families could afford the extra few pounds. One in particular I remember was, 'Cyril, dear Cyril, our beautiful son'. I wondered how his parents had ached to hold his fine young body lying within this French soil. It reminded me of the Michelangelo *Pietà*, and Mary holding the dead, limp body of Christ. Cyril's parents, like the majority of parents, did not have that last, grief-stricken opportunity to hold the body of their son or even visit his grave.

Perhaps in some small way, in my ability to be there, I could acknowledge him on their behalf.

As a mother of sons, one at the time of the visit serving in Iraq, the tour was particularly poignant. I yearned and prayed for his safety, lit candles in many places and lived for four months in a state of unease. After the Somme visit, I thanked God for his safe return and rejoiced in holding him, young and vital.

Where was God in that battle in 1916? Perhaps in the many acts of bravery and courage. Certainly in the deep bonds of comradeship and brotherly love among the soldiers. And undoubtedly with them, in their profound suffering and the brokenness of their youthful bodies. Yes, God was there, mourning his sons and the destructiveness of man's inhumanity to man.

Shelley Wild

13

God in the midst of life

Introduction

If God is love, as the Christian gospel proclaims, then wherever love is God is. Wherever love shows itself, there is God to be known. Wherever we recognize, are encountered and overwhelmed by love, there we have been met by God. It is as simple as that.

Falling in love with another human being, in whatever way that may happen, is very like falling in love with God: indeed, it is a falling in love with God. The pattern is much the same: the initial wonder and excitement, the perception of the other as perfect and without flaw, the longing to be with the other always and the consequent pain at separation; and the rosy view of the rest of life that all this engenders, followed by the gradual realization that it is not all quite so simple, and that the other does have failings, faults and habits that irritate. They do not, and indeed appear to be neither able or willing, to meet all our needs. There are sometimes some almighty misunderstandings and arguments, not to say rows! It is sometimes good to be apart from them. Love is a hard, demanding slog for much of the time.

And all of this is true of both our human relationships and our relationship with this loving God who seeks relationship with us. No wonder so many of our pop songs, which deal with the ups and downs of falling in and out of love, actually make rather good prayers and hymns. Why do specialist hymn writers bother, I sometimes wonder? It's all there in the love songs of the age.

OK, I hear the counter-argument: God's love is distinctly different, richer and deeper than anything we can receive from another human being, and that religious experience requires, demands

185

even, a special category of verse and prose to describe it adequately. I agree that there is truth in that. But I still maintain my point. If God is love, then wherever love meets us then there we are encountered by God, and to fail to recognize this, to restrict the love of God to a special compartment of our lives into which other parts of our lives may not enter, is significantly to misrepresent the God of whom Christianity speaks. Our faith talks, does it not, of an incarnational God: a God who gets involved with the messy business of human living and reveals God-self through it and in the life of a particular human being. Our reflections earlier of the God who meets us through the pages of the Bible led us straight to such a God: one who rejects being found only in the special religious activities of the few, and insists on encountering us through the everyday and the ordinary. A God like that, who seeks us in a relationship of love, cannot but be met significantly in our loving human relationships. Surely it cannot be otherwise?

So learning, from life's humblest beginnings to its uncertain end, to receive and to give love, is not only of the essence of being human, but being so, it is also where we most simply encounter and are encountered by God. In learning to cope with love's failures, regrets and mistakes, we may grow more deeply into love with the Source of Love itself. We move from one incarnation of God's love to another, and are most often surrounded by many of them, for the loving God incarnates God-self in love in every relationship we enter.

One of my favourite prayer exercises is to remember and celebrate all those people it's been my pleasure and privilege to love and to receive love from, throughout my life: these are the men and woman who have incarnated God to me over and over again. They may not have done it perfectly – I certainly have not done it perfectly – but I salute them as sons and daughters of the God of love. Interestingly, it's probably best that none of us has done it perfectly, for if we had we would think that we had nothing else to learn and would almost certainly fall into pride. And one of the hallmarks of incarnational love is its humility.

For this chapter I invited a number of our friends to reflect on the nature of relationships, on what they have learnt from them and where and how God has been encountered through them. I've asked others to look at particular important areas of life. There is one piece on liminal space, which is followed by two examples of people entering such a time, as one left a convent and another began retirement.

Some of these experiences you may know personally but may reflect differently on them; others may be new to you. We are not suggesting that these reflections offer *the* way to reflect on these things, and each writer could surely have said more given the opportunity, but they offer *a* way. Hopefully these contributions will stimulate deeper and renewed reflection on your own experience. You might like to write something for your own personal benefit. And if you'd like to send it by email to Roy and myself (see <www.annunciationtrust.org.uk/>) we'll be pleased to consider adding it to the Annunciation Trust website for others to read and perhaps be inspired by.

HM

Sexuality

Finding a home for all our desires is one of the challenges on a spiritual path. We desire many things that we are told are not wholesome or grown-up. What has been true in our culture is that it has been difficult to make a home big enough to hold our desires for God and our sexual desires.

The word 'sexuality' can have a number of meanings bound up with identity and desire:

- *Gender*: male, female, transsexual, trans-gender . . .
- *Orientation*: straight, gay/lesbian, bisexual . . .
- *Relationship status*: single, married, civil partnership, celibate . . .
- *Desire*: for physical contact with one or more people, for solitude . . .

In each of these, the church has guidelines for what is OK: certain forms of sexuality are acceptable; others less so, even 'intrinsically disordered'. Those who fall outside these guidelines (and I suspect this is all of us, for we all desire what is not 'allowed') may harbour a number of reactions:

- I may feel guilty and ashamed of my sexuality.
- I may feel alienation from the group of those I perceive as being pure and free from wayward desires and lifestyles.
- I may think something is wrong with me.
- I may grow angry and rejecting towards God, towards those who make pronouncements about what and who I should be, or towards myself.

A conflict arises between sexual desire and desire for God. And yet so many of the same words are used for both; classical spiritual writings often talk about desire for God with the same language as the desire for a human lover. The Song of Songs is a classic example.

William Blake wrote: 'Sooner murder an infant in its cradle than nurse unacted desires' ('The Marriage of Heaven and Hell'). It seems to me that we have to walk a narrow path between murdering the infant of our desires (squashing and ignoring them) and nursing our desires (indulging and acting them out). It is simply not possible to rid ourselves of desires. To try to do so is a kind of violence, and there is already enough of that in the world. Homemaking of the soul means to welcome all our desires, for those desires we turn away from the door or put in a box in the cupboard have a way of coming in by other doors, unannounced. Only when a desire is welcomed into the home can responses and choices for action be discerned.

We fear that if we admit to our sexual desires, we will sully ourselves, or that action will necessarily follow. Neither of these things is the case. So, what to do?

The most important step is to be myself honestly with God – to be gentle, tender and compassionate with myself, trusting in God's love, acceptance, understanding and desire. The usual things are helpful in this: praying, journalling, drawing, sharing with a friend, and so on. What can help is allowing my desire to have a home in me, feeling it in my body and, prayerfully, meeting it with compassionate silence. Then I have the possibility of being a home where the whole family can live in peace.

This is not to ask and hope for change. How am I to know what change to hope for? It is simply no longer to separate who I am from God. In truth, I neither know who I am, nor do I know that God loves who I am, but God knows who I am and loves me. I must trust that God will do with me, with my sexuality, what gives me life.

Julian Maddock

Celibacy

Celibacy isn't for the faint-hearted. It's for the wholehearted who want to include as many people as possible in their loving. For me, it isn't about absence, or avoidance, it's all about inclusion and risk. And passion. Is that a bit shocking? Surprising? Positive?

I am talking about chosen celibacy, in the context of a religious community of Anglican sisters, deep in the East End of London. The context in which I live out celibacy is important, as it forms one of the vows that a sister takes at profession, or life commitment. I have lived in community for 20 years. I continue to be a sexual being, as everyone is, but I choose not to express this genitally.

I am aware that celibacy in this day and age is counter-cultural, and can be viewed as something that 'sad' people end up doing because they can't find a partner. It can be seen as a failure of some kind, or something imposed. It may be surprising to realize that some of us, men and women, choose it as a form of life that suits us best. I don't think it works if it's chosen to avoid sex or deny sexuality or because no other opportunity arises, but I can only speak from my own experience. This doesn't mean it's an easy option if it's a positive choice. There can be moments of intense alone-ness and questioning – I wasn't joking about the faint-hearted. Those are the moments I know that God is ultimately all I have, and I need to trust a lot more than I might be doing in that moment. It can be a painful place of self-revelation. Prayer doesn't allow you to lie to yourself about what or how you are feeling and why you are feeling it.

So, having chosen this path, what does it mean for me? Sexuality and spirituality are closely linked, and one of the elements I believe links them together is passion. Your treasure is where your heart is, and it's that driving energy that needs using well. So my choice is, where do I put my passion, or energy and enthusiasm, in response to the invitation of God to be the human being that I am meant to be, and to help build the kingdom here and now? The key lies in where my focus is. Again and again I am drawn back to God. He/She is irresistible. There lies my passion. Because of who I am, if I were to be focused exclusively on the happiness and well-being of one person I couldn't give much attention elsewhere. I would be quite distracted. For others it is quite the opposite, and living in an exclusive partnership enables them to embrace God more fully. Ideally, what celibacy does is give me the freedom to give of myself in various places in my day-to-day life, whether in community living or in my ministry outside the house. It opens me up to other people rather than closing me down. It's a liberating choice, letting me be as generous as I can with my time, attention and energy, and it certainly doesn't mean that I can't have deep friendships – I have close friends, both men and women, who are very important to me and my sanity!

The risk is that to grow I have to keep choosing to be open-hearted, and that leads to a certain vulnerability, but I think it has been a risk worth taking, which for me has led to joy.

Sue Makin

Civil partnership

I share William Stringfellow's practice of not regarding prayer and words as especially related or mutually dependent; indeed, I share his view that much of what passes for Christian prayer is inimical to its true character. I view prayer as a mixture of attitude, method and action. It is not that I don't use words, at times, as prayer: I used them only the other day when undergoing a surgical procedure that made me anxious, and I still make explicit and urgent requests for help when fearful or distressed, for myself or another.

This mixture of attitude, method and action will not surprise those who have seriously thought about prayer. The *attitude* arises from the context, which for me is a decision to live in the belief that God 'is', and 'is' as pointed to by Jesus in the Gospels and by the most persuasive parts of the tradition. The *method* is to view all that I do as either contributing to God's way of doing things, or frustrating that. It applies to any and everything, from cooking a meal to running a multi-million-pound organization. And the place of *action* seems to me important. I don't mean it in any 'Action Man' way of heroics but simply the claim that what we say we believe is either affirmed or contradicted by what we do.

And 'prayer' can surprise us by making its presence apparent when it's the last thing we think we are doing. A little while ago Stephen and I registered our civil partnership, soon after this became possible in England for same-sex couples. We had lived together for 16 years and had much earlier reached the stage, which many will recognize, of loving each other in ways that are deep, familiar, challenging, reassuring, full of gentleness and humour; ways that have both the sense of real permanence *and* the freshness of a gift newly received every day. We were supported by a network of friends. We had no special need of the state's recognition, but saw it as a wise step in order to protect the other by acquiring the various rights (such as next-of-kin status) that marriage gives those who are permitted to enter it.

The actual experience of our civil partnership – the event of the ceremony and the subsequent effects of that step – were far and away far, far more significant than I had expected, and as I now see it, above all else, an act of prayer. The state allows no 'religious' texts but we had slipped in under the registrar's radar Thomas à Kempis' writing on the nature of love. The making of public promises to each other turned out to have a reality and an impact I had not expected. I am unable to explain this, except to note these elements. Over the years we have been together, I had made promises to Stephen and he to me, occasionally explicit but mostly implicit through the 'simple' business of loving one another. Now, the state was willing to hear and recognize these promises, and to confer upon us the same rights and obligations the majority take for granted. There was a powerful sense of 'attitude, method and action' – the elements I regard as present in prayer – coming together. I cannot convey the joy or significance for us, or the sense that this was, in that serviceable Quaker phrase, 'in right ordering'. In *very* 'right ordering'. The fact that the church, in its institutional form, had adopted a position of disdain towards its gay and lesbian sons and daughters undertaking such a step was merely a regret rather than an affront, for the church in its essential character – its baptized members – was present. This officially illicit (but actually real) part of the Body of Christ was met in a municipal registry office to celebrate the greatest of God's sacraments, the one that the Thomas à Kempis reading concisely expressed in its very first sentence: 'Love is a great power, a great and complete good.'

Hugh Valentine

Marriage

Marriage is one of the toughest spiritual paths around. It's a struggle; the rewards are immeasurable.

I'm not very good at being married – at the sharing and negotiating involved – and my current wife is not my first. I am an introvert; my wife is an extrovert; we have children: I struggle to balance intimacy, responsibility and solitude. Having God as a third person in a marriage isn't always helpful: where one might look to the other for pleasure and support, I also look to God and want time with God. I struggle with all this.

Having lived alone for significant chunks of my life, learning to share my life – decisions, space, money – is an unfolding of where love and justice take me. For example: I work full-time and earn all the money. This is a decision we took so that our pre-school children have a full-time parent. I had to struggle to be generous enough to put all 'my' money into a common account and to lose control over how it was spent: how money is dealt with is emblematic of many aspects of a relationship. I think there are two fundamental challenges in any committed relationship. The first is to learn about and delve into being together, to find out what it means to be a couple, that 'these two are now one'. Other people, and my spouse in particular, think, pray and act differently from me. This leads me into a bigger world, one with a broader acceptance. It is a world of homemaking, of fitting around and together, of learning about and accommodating difference, of dealing with the wounds from our first families. It is slowly coming to see that this other *is* God, *is* Christ: she or he *is* what God is doing in my life. It is the comfort of presence: this warm body *is* God present, here, now.

Some of the most graced moments are when I uncover some deeply pained part of myself and I bring it, with cupped hands, honestly to another who receives it with complete acceptance: here is the crucial connection and identity between the other who is my spouse and the Other who is God.

I used to cherish time alone as my time with God. I still do, but now I know much more clearly that God *is* always and everywhere, and that every moment is an opportunity to recognize and act within this. If one has lived alone for some time, perhaps it is letting in another person and losing oneself that is the greater challenge. My life is not about me. I am not that important.

The second challenge is to find out who I am as an individual. I remain forever a loved child of God, a creature 'on a kind of extended emergency bivouac' (Annie Dillard, *Pilgrim at Tinker Creek*) and I still have my own journey of discovery and homecoming to make. It is a growing realization that God *is* me, that there is nowhere else to go. Rilke warns against lovers who 'keep on using each other to hide their own fate' (*Duino Elegy No. 1*). If one marries early, or has never lived alone, the first challenge is the formative process and the second comes later. I have met people who married young, have never had a night apart, and for whom the separation due to illness, ageing and death reveals a gaping lack of identity.

Either way, there is a lot of dying to be gone through if one is to undertake marriage with integrity. To strive to be whole both as an individual and a couple is an achievement.

Julian Maddock

Married to a Hindu

I married a wonderful guy who happened to be Hindu, which took me and many of my more conventional evangelical Christian friends by surprise. It was not the thing I was taught would progress my Christian walk, but it has. It took me to a place of finding 'my God' rather than one that was passed on to me by others, however well-meaning. My God, I have discovered, wants us to be happy, to live according to his word as best we can without the burden of guilt.

I find my prayer life richer for having married a Hindu. I tend not to be complacent about needing God in my and our lives. It is just down to me to ensure that the regular prayer happens.

I go to the Hindu temple with my husband and children as well as to my own church. We had a naming ceremony in the temple and a blessing in my church. All the family attended both. I can remember, early on in our life together, sitting in the temple thinking, 'What do I do now?' and deciding that I had to take responsibility for my own faith journey.

Being a Christian (however you may define it) and marrying a Hindu has brought challenges to my Christian life. People ask if I would have done things differently. I fell in love and I see God in our marriage; what else could I ask for?

We do not pray together as a couple. My husband would not want to and our interpretations of faith and prayer are very different. Sometimes it seems recognizing and respecting difference can bring more unity than some false sense of praying together just because a Christian group or tradition says it is a 'good thing to do'. I have never asked my husband to come to church, and when he has come it has been of his own volition and this works better for us. In fact at church, because, I guess, it is less intense, I do feel we can be side by side and 'pray together'.

I ask God to be with me when I visit my husband's temple and that God will be walking alongside the children. I pray with my little boy every night, to thank God for the day and to bring any worries he may have to his Father's feet. And yes, I do pray for my husband but not in an incessant, obsessive way. I simply ask that he may know God as I do, whatever form that may look like to the outside world. I have learnt to leave all that to God.

In writing this, I have realized that being married to someone of another faith has strengthened my own by taking me on a journey that few I know have embarked on. I have needed to find my own ways to maintain and strengthen my faith and prayer life. It has pushed me to go beyond my own evangelical background to explore other ways of finding and relating to God. I have also learnt to appreciate my husband's faith and his Hindu faith community. It has strengthened my appreciation of church, since coming to church, often on my own, can be like 'coming home' and a precious place for me.

Stephanie Shah

Motherhood

My journey to motherhood and subsequent experience of it has taken me to emotional limits, expanding my sense of self. It was nine years after we started trying for a baby that our eldest was born and we waited a further five years for our twins. These were years full of hope and despair in equal measure as we experienced the wonders and traumas of intrusive medical attention and the heartache of two miscarriages.

The drive towards motherhood was, for me, overwhelming. Ongoing failure to fulfil the impulse was charged with questions about my womanhood and sense of purpose in life. These are not logical but entirely emotional and no less significant because of that. There were times of overpowering darkness, the sort that might smother and destroy. The struggle for me was not to go under but to come out the other end, whatever the result, not only in one piece but stronger. There were the obvious feelings of hurt and sadness, failure and powerlessness; the pressure of living with uncertainty, always hoping but never being sure. These were painful emotions but the real demons were those lurking in my shadow side with which I became increasingly familiar: feelings of jealousy, rage and resentment. I was ever conscious that these had the power to destroy and embitter me. I did not want that to be the sum of my life and I prayed for the strength to be spared this.

In all this, God was never far away. Not as an all-powerful miracle-maker but a loving presence: holding, carrying, being alongside me. I grew increasingly conscious of a God who had put creation into motion before standing back, allowing it to take its course, freely and without restraint, sometimes for better, sometimes for worse. I was feeling the downside of God's gift of free will through the limiting of his powers in creation. In life, I believe, there is good and there is bad but there is always the possibility for good to grow out of evil. So while, of course, I beseeched God to hear my plea, at a deeper level I prayed for strength to bear the burden. And all the while a still small voice within me whispered that I should be patient and that all would be well. I hoped for a wish fulfilled but clung on, in trust, to the notion that something after all would fill the void; if not motherhood, then something else.

In the event, on a Wednesday afternoon shortly before Holy Week, my long Good Friday gave way to Easter morn. The elation of motherhood and the relative calm of a house with one small child has, since the arrival of our twins, developed into deep contentment, notwithstanding the chaos, noise and disorder that are an inevitable part of life at this stage. There is little time for quiet reflection or focused spirituality but there are moments in which my life makes complete sense and glimpses of how perfectly faith can sustain me. Once again I encounter new emotional boundaries: anger and frustration can in an instant give way to overwhelming love. The potency of these emotions is for me particular to my experience of motherhood and I wonder whether they mirror something of the nature of God's love for us.

There is all too little emphasis on the motherhood of God in the Christian tradition, yet it offers rich potential. One persistent theme stresses the sacrificial nature of God being like that of a mother. Sacrifice suggests something that is painful and difficult, involving a heavy cost. Yet at its best, a mother's sacrifice is borne willingly. Love for my children and the pleasure they give me can replace or at least surmount the worry and guilt, the pain of letting go, the frustration of losing my sense of identity and all the other difficult emotions that go with motherhood.

My brother died when he was 24 and I have watched my mother live with the loss of a child. It is perhaps the hardest pain and has made me more conscious of the fragility of life and how we can never possess our children. My three are gifts for me to cherish and nurture and I hope that they in turn will travel life's journey free of constraint but in the knowledge that they are loved. My children have given me the gift of contentment, thus bringing out the best in me. Yet motherhood is a humbling experience that also continually exposes my weaknesses and failings. Each night I pray that despite my shortcomings my children will grow to be happy and secure. For through it all I love them with a passion that reflects for me something of the wonder of God's love for her creation.

Guli Francis-Dehqani

Fatherhood

Life with two young children now aged five and three has been exhilarating, exhausting, stimulating and challenging and has given me some of the richest, most intense experiences of God I have ever known. Having children has left no part of my life untouched – it affects everything, from the time I wake up in the morning, how I drive (more defensively), the clothes I wear (baby sick is notoriously difficult to get out of clerical corduroy), and what I eat. It doesn't seem too strong to talk about the experience as a kind of conversion.

Not much of my experience through this particular conversion has had much to do either with church or with spending long periods of time in silent contemplation. This is fortunate because small children (or mine anyway) aren't especially given to tolerating long services in church, still less spending time in silent contemplation. There are many different features of my conversion and here I want to touch on just two: dispossession and delight.

The experience of dispossession has been an important part of what my children have brought to me, and their presence in dependence and independence profoundly challenges my sense of self-possession, the ownership I think I have of my own time, energy and resources. In one sense my children are highly dependent and need me in some pretty concrete ways to help them do even basic tasks. This kind of dependence forces me to abandon a picture of myself as an autonomous, self-possessed individual. At the same time my children are highly independent in many ways; they are not simply clones of me, we don't think alike on many issues(!) and they have their own priorities, friends, likes and dislikes. Their independence thus resists fiercely any possibility of my turning them into my possessions, of owning them.

Dispossession, at times, has been a painful process, as the truth that children bring exposes my limitations, selfishness and self-centredness. The surprise, though, is how joyful much of this process is, a willing dispossession which, though not particularly voluntary, enlarges and enriches me, eliciting reserves of energy, patience and love that I didn't know existed before. I am sure that God chooses many different ways to prise us away from our obsessive owning of things in order to learn to love, and being dispossessed by the presence of your children is but one.

If all this sounds a little negative, there are many times when I take delight in my children. My most powerful experiences of delight are when I see them enjoying themselves and utterly absorbed or lost in what they are doing. They have an ability to focus with a single-minded abandon which awes me and of which I am envious. If only, I think, I had something of that same focus and abandonment before God.

My experience of delight is not the same as feeling proud of them or willing them on to do or achieve something; it's somehow deeper and more intense than those other feelings. It leaves me wondering when it is that God most delights in me. Does God most delight in me when I am busy achieving things, leading worship, or serving others? My experience with my own children suggests that God most delights in me when I am taken out of myself, lost and absorbed in something I enjoy doing, however trivial or serious. For someone who is strongly motivated by ideals of service, duty and achievement this is a severe challenge.

My children remind me that God's love for me and delight in me does not depend upon my achievements, that beyond every calculation of merit or desert, I am loved and delighted in.

Of course, experiences of dispossession and delight are not unique to parent–child relationships but are part of all of our significant relationships. However, my children have focused these experiences for me with a clarity and intensity I hadn't known before. There is still much I need to learn about being dispossessed by a God in whose service is perfect freedom, and delighted in by my Creator in whose image I am made.

James Grenfell

Being a granddad

Spending time with young children, as an older person, is reward-ing and beneficial in ways that I have found surprising. It is just great to have excuses to play, to tell stories that move so easily into complete fantasy with a captivated audience. We can fly or see fairies or have whole families of pretend animals who all talk and do unusual things. This, for me, is something of the freedom of being a child that Jesus spoke about. It brings me a new sense of God's kingdom by releasing my imagination and allowing me to enjoy all of life's possibilities. It is not an exaggeration to say that being with my grandchildren is for me a prayer that touches the very character of God.

The whole experience of being 'a granddad' was itself a com-plete surprise to me even though, since my wife and I have children of our own, it should have been anticipated!

Reflecting on this now I realize that grandparents did not fea-ture greatly in my family experience. I suppose it was not some-thing I had thought about before. I only knew one of mine and she died when I was five. Our children only knew one of theirs who died when they were quite young too.

Possibly the experience of having three granddaughters has been all the more powerful and precious because of this. On the debit side I have seen what I missed, but this is far outweighed by the current experience. I remember the day I realized that I was entering into a new relationship. Since I had not known a grand-dad of my own I found I could make up my own version of the role. This has been a creative and interesting time unhindered by any baggage from the past. I have found it stimulating and freeing.

My granddaughters are eighteen months, three and four as I write and are, of course, all totally beautiful and delightful! I share with my wife some of the childminding responsibilities on a day-to-day basis. I have watched the effortless learning of language, seen the great inbuilt desire to learn and develop and create relationships. It has been truly awe-inspiring although, of course, I did see this before in my own children. Somehow, second time round, these things are more emphasized by having more time to be with them and also by realizing how short is this part of their lives and hence how important it is to grab every moment.

It was a while ago when I realized that having grandchildren in my mid sixties means that there is a good possibility that I will not live to see them as adults. This was different from my own children, where I expected to see them grow up and could to some extent look forward to an adult relationship and hence did not always value what was happening in the moment. With my grand-children the relationship I have is 'it' and I value it the more for that. It has helped me to live 'in the moment' and I have found that a spiritually rewarding experience.

Young grandchildren have added a new dimension to being unconditionally loved for who I am. Perhaps part of this special appreciation is due to my age. At a time when inevitably roles are reducing in terms of career it is somehow amazing that the little person just wants you to be around and squeals with delight to see you – not because you are clever, powerful or wise, but just because you are her granddad. A very moving experience of un-conditional love easily translated into God's love for us.

RG

Relationships

I am a church pastor and value church and all that it can do for me and for others. I have spent a good deal of my adult life trying to make church the best experience I can for all who come. I believe that for me it is important, but if I had to *choose*, rather than a church service, I would opt for an evening with a good friend or friends talking about faith. When the 'chips are down' I would go to family and friends to find God.

I can recall the experience of coming to this startling conclusion. I had just finished conducting a service in the church I belong to and I felt it had gone well with a sense of God's presence. It was a week when the church stayed to lunch together so there was work to be done in the kitchen and I was happy to be there generally helping. As the group of us worked together and laughed together, I realized that this was even better than the service!

Looking back at that moment, I understood that it helped me to see that some of my own struggles with church were not really about the church, but arose because I went to church primarily for relationship and interactions with people of faith. Sometimes the church service gets in the way of the interactions I personally need. Often the standard sermon, whether preached by me or someone else, can be quite frustrating when what I really want to do to find God is to talk and discuss with other people. I find myself just waiting for the coffee time to find God!

To me the relational space between people is sacred space and God is there in the humanity of that relationship. I am always moved at airports when friends, families and lovers greet each other, and the masks of restraint slip for a moment to show the sacred space that relationships occupy. The hugs, the kisses, the squeals of delight, celebrate something of what it is to be human and hence something of the God who made us.

I have been a pastor and a spiritual director for many years and have come to see that my interactions with others form one of my significant sacred spaces. It brings me close to God and to a type of worshipful prayer, as words are used to express the inexpressible, and through the words, analogies and metaphors God shows through. I invariably receive more than I give during these encounters. I receive something of the incarnational Christian God through others, which I believe is reflected in the sayings of Jesus such as: 'I tell you the truth, whatever you did not do for one of the least of these, you did not do for me' (Matthew 25.45, NIV) and, 'For where two or three come together in my name, there am I with them' [Matthew 18.20, NIV). These verses resonate with my experience that relationship and interaction with others touch God.

Relaxing into this realization has made for an exciting time. It has changed the way that I preach now, with much more interaction, so that 'preaching' is probably not the right word any more for what I do. I have found that I am happier preaching like this.

Also, God can appear through others at any time and place: in the supermarket, in the pub, at work, on the train, and at the airport. God can appear when human beings reach out to each other in their humanity. A railway station, a hospital, a market stall can all be sacred places.

RG

Entering 'liminal space'

Some years ago I felt myself to be called by God to leave parish ministry in order to explore a different way of being a priest. At a weekend I led for another parish I remember being introduced as 'a man who is about to jump off a cliff', and indeed it felt very like that. Here I was leaving a job, a house, a stipend and a pension, just about everything, and for what? I could not have told you, because I was not at all clear myself. All I had was this strong sense that this was what God was calling me to do. It felt very scary. But it also felt as if God had me in a corner and there was really nowhere else for me to go. So I jumped off the cliff. Most people thought I was crazy, but friends gave me their trust and support.

These liminal times come to many of us at some point in our lives. We are clear what we *don't* feel is the right thing to do; we sense that we might be being called to do something else, but we often can't name what it is, we can't see it. We are being called to let go and to trust: trust our own inner voice, our own intuition, the voice of God, call it what you will. It feels scary: having just to wait and to trust, and to live with the not knowing. The temptation is to go back to the familiar, to stay with what we know. The temptation is to rush to fill the empty space with solutions and frantic activity.

These liminal times come in all manner of ways. They may, as I found, come in mid-life, when we become aware that life is nearly half over, death and old age await us, and we are not at all sure that we're in the right place and doing what we feel we should be. Perhaps we find ourselves asking the questions about the meaning of life, and of what God might be calling us to be, that we had last wrestled with when we were much younger.

They may happen because tragedy strikes and we face loss in one form or another; we are struck down by a serious illness; an important relationship comes to an end and we have to face the future on our own. They may happen because we lose our job or an important role we held. They may happen at retirement. They often happen to women when their children start school, or leave home, and suddenly there is a space to find themselves once again, or even for the first time!

They may be fuelled by a deepening sense of frustration, anger even, that where we are in our lives right now is simply not right. It sometimes seems as if we need a head of anger to build up in us to get us to face the possibility of taking the risk and trying something else. Or they may be fuelled by a vision we have that simply won't go away and that we know deep down we have to honour.

However they come, they are rarely of our conscious choosing. It seems as if something comes from outside of us and seeks to take us over. We have then to choose whether or not we follow it. Whether or not to trust. Whether to trust ourselves and God, because they are often two sides of the same coin. Put like that a liminal time is, of course, a gift, but it doesn't feel like that when it comes and we are in the midst of it. And perhaps it may be right to let it pass by: to know that this is not the right time for us, or that we are not yet ready; this also is possible.

HM

203

Sabbatical space

I had been thinking for some time about giving myself a sabbatical of three months, and as I'm self-employed I can technically do that more easily than most. I say technically, because it isn't that easy to set aside three months when you know that you won't be generating any income, and to trust that it will be OK. But I sensed that God was calling me to do this, so encouraged by friends I took the plunge.

First of all I put a line through three months in next year's diary: that was going to be my sabbatical space. Then I asked myself, 'What would I like to do during that time?' I could do whatever I wanted. There was nothing I had to do. And a bit to my surprise I quickly found that I could make a list of over half a dozen things I wanted to do on my sabbatical. Even more surprising, I found that when I had written this list, it was as if someone flicked a switch on inside me and I felt a surge of creative energy rising up within me at the prospect of being free to do these things.

The sabbatical was still almost a year ahead of me. But I discovered that marking off the time in my diary and making a list of how I might use it began a very creative process in me. It gave me permission to begin to do some of the things on that list *now*. In fact, by the time the sabbatical began I had either done the things on my list or they had ceased to seem important. Other things had emerged that actually were what I spent my time with during my precious three months. Moreover, during the months before my sabbatical began, all sorts of bits of synchronicity occurred, as ideas and intuitions surfaced within as to what deep down I needed to do on sabbatical.

I had had a sabbatical before, many years ago, I add defensively! And I'd talked quite a lot of people through sabbaticals, so I knew some of the basic advice:

1 You will be surprised at how tired you feel when it begins. We keep going until we stop, and then suddenly the weariness catches up with us. The wisdom is that you have to let your

body recover, and don't try to do anything much until your body tells you that it is ready. You will have no difficulty recognizing when this occurs. I know this, but I still found it frustrating when I had had nearly six weeks of sabbatical and still had no real energy for anything. But quite suddenly it lifted, and I was then amazed by how much happened in the time remaining.

2 It's good to start with a holiday, to mark to yourself and to others that you are entering a different period of time.

3 It's good to have one project prepared for your sabbatical, but leave plenty of space around it, because the really interesting things probably won't surface in your consciousness until the sabbatical is under way, and you will need time and energy to attend to them when they occur.

4 Plan to give yourself a few days off about two or three months after the sabbatical is over. Let this be a time when you can look back on your sabbatical and wonder again at what it taught you. One of the deadliest problems with a sabbatical is that within a week or two of being back in the old routines you will find that you have forgotten all the wise advice you learnt on your sabbatical. So these few days will give you an opportunity to stop that happening.

Ideally, of course, once your sabbatical is over, you decide when you will have your next one, and then you make a list . . .

Now you are probably saying to yourself, with some exasperation, that this is all very well for people who can take several months off, but you simply cannot do that. But you can, you can! You may not be able to take three months off. But you can surely give yourself one day a week off, or a couple of hours a week, or half an hour each day? There is a biblical principle, remember, of having one sabbath day each week.

And you surely can start to make a list of what you'd like to do if you did have three months. And having named those things to yourself, there is surely nothing stopping you (except yourself) from beginning to do some of those things in a small way now.

HM

205

Leaving the convent

Eight years ago I was living in a convent, and struggling. It was the wrong place for me: I felt isolated and at odds with the people with whom I was supposed to be living in communion. I was fighting a daily battle against my own unexpressed anger, which threatened to plunge me deep into depression. I experienced black despair, panic and chronic insomnia, which left me exhausted. I needed to leave, but was terrified that I wouldn't be able to cope alone.

Living in a convent, prayer was never an optional extra. How many times did I drag myself to the oratory, to mouth words I didn't mean and resented having to use? Did the real prayer happen at night – alone in the silence: the anger, the fear and the desolation laid before God? Again and again in my journal for that period, I come across the words: 'underneath are the everlasting arms' (Deuteronomy 33.27). I clung to the belief that God was holding me: always there.

Eventually, inevitably, I reached the point of deciding to leave. The only reason I had not done so sooner was my terror of stepping out into the unknown alone. Despite fear, the decision felt right. When I entered the community, I saw it as a handing over of myself to God; leaving felt as though God was handing that self back to me willingly. Still, it was hard. As well as the practical issues of finding somewhere to live, finding a job, coping with financial insecurity, there was the emotional insecurity of being completely alone in a strange place. I had never lived alone before, and I didn't know if I could do it: I just knew I had to try.

Initially I sought out church as a means of establishing contact with people rather than maintaining contact with God. I didn't really know how much contact with God I actually wanted. Stuck on the wall of my bedsit I had the words: 'Be still and know . . .' (Psalm 46.10). A Christian friend asked me why I had not completed the quotation: '. . . that I am God.' I tried to explain that I did not need, or want, God to be spelt out. God is implicit in the knowing, as God is implicit in all things; there was no need to draw attention to that. I was not praying at that time. I attended church sporadically, often finding that it made me homesick for what I had left. There were times (there still are) when I was angry with God; there were also times when I wasn't even sure that God existed at all. Yet I still needed God. One of my earliest acquisitions was a prayer book, though it was some time before I was ready to use it. Even when I thought I didn't believe in God, I must have been still, at some level, aware of those 'everlasting arms' holding me. It didn't matter that I couldn't pray: God took care of that for me. I say that because, looking back, I find that I have forgotten just how painful the experience really was: rereading my journal for that time was actually something of a shock. What I remember is the positive: the generosity of so many people who helped kit out my tiny kitchen; the encouragement and support of friends; the fact that I did survive and learn to enjoy living alone; and the warmth of the relationship that I still have with the sisters in the convent.

Lynn Terrell

Retirement

I'm writing this piece six months after retiring from a management post in a public sector organization. I hadn't intended to retire quite when I did, but following yet another reconfiguration of the management structure I felt it was time to cut loose and see where I would be led. Being given the space and opportunity a few years earlier than I had expected was my big chance to find out.

As I write, I'm perched with my laptop in a tiny room on a residential weekend designed to introduce the mysteries of Christian theology to a group of ministry students, of which I'm now a part. I'm on another journey, quite different from the one in the world of 'real' work, and one whose destination is as yet unknown to me.

Leaving work behind and adjusting to a new way of being has not been without its challenges. I've enjoyed work's rough and tumble with its human relationships and the feeling of 'making a difference'. But even as I've grieved for the loss of my role, I'm becoming alert to new possibilities. God has always been around in my life to a greater or lesser degree but often I've shut him out, wilfully refusing to acknowledge that he's knocking on the door. It's been more convenient somehow – after all, who knows what I'd be given to do if I turned fully and looked him in the face! Yet here I am on my doorstep daring to enter into dialogue with the one who's so persistently tried to get in.

In letting go and entering into the Space, with time and trust, both new and long-buried forms are emerging into my consciousness. In my former life, I was at the helm and firmly in control. My work life, and by virtue of this my personal and family life, was well constrained and directed by the requirements of the job. Hence I could create valid reasons to ignore God's invitations – I just couldn't fit him into my busy schedule! In my reflective moments I now sense that God has despaired at my rebuffs and so has been instrumental in creating the space for me to accept his invitation. This makes me sound more important than I feel; why should God be at all bothered with little me? Only God knows the answer to that one, but his persistence is very seductive and his call is becoming increasingly hard to resist.

So here I stand on the edge of the Space. I'm well versed in planning; it would be easy to revert to old habits and create the God Project to fill the space. It would be easy to jump into any number of new ventures and goodness knows there are many to choose from. But I risk squeezing him out again if I do this. So I won't. With his support I'll wait. And listen.

Joanna Finegan

Vocation

I grew up with a real awareness of God. It's easy to connect with the Creator when you live on a farm. I guess you could say that my sense of vocation first grew out of that awareness of God who creates: creation has a purpose. We are all born with our 'purpose' deep within us, and as we grow and develop we discover more about how we can live this 'purpose'.

As an adult I grappled with trying to understand what vocation was, and specifically what I was called to. It began to feel a bit like being one of those Russian dolls – you know, the painted, placid-faced beauties, each of which opens up to reveal another, slightly smaller doll nested inside. I felt called to be different things, which sometimes didn't seem to sit together very comfortably. Sometimes I questioned whether I could really have 'got it right' when I found that compromises were inevitable: what about my calling as a mother when my job meant I couldn't always be at the parent–teacher meeting? Could I really make the vocations to which I felt called fit together?

Sometimes it's easy to compartmentalize life, to think that vocation is only about priesthood, or the part of our lives where we are 'doing something for God'. I have a card I keep that reminds me that 'I am not a human doing'; vocation is much deeper than just what we do, it's about who we are created by God to be. It's part of the pattern of all of our lives: all of us are called by God to be ourselves. We can get a sense of vocation when we become aware of the things that we do, or the events we become involved in that seem to give us life. But sometimes fear of change (or fear of commitment) can stop us from moving in the direction that deep down feels life-giving: we have a choice whether or not to try our vocation.

Vocation itself seems to me to be more like being part of a complex dance, where joining in means taking the risk that maybe our steps won't be quite right until we've learnt how to move, and felt in our souls the rhythm of the music that called us. It isn't that each calling or vocation exists on its own; somehow they all interplay, affecting each other in a complex and intricate way. I'm a different priest because I'm also a mother, and my way of bringing up my children has always been affected by my understanding of the importance of the spiritual. There's an intermingling, and a movement back and forth. To use the dance analogy again, sometimes one theme in the music we dance to is more dominant, sometimes another, but all have their irreplaceable parts in the whole performance.

Annabel Barber

The solitary life

As an inveterate pusher of boundaries, I moved, over a number of years, from a position of sincere orthodoxy to an unsettling search for truth that made sense in the light of my own experience. In the synchronous way in which these things happen, I kept coming across references to the simplicity, silence and solitude that make up the life of a solitary. This life cannot, in one sense, be described because it is expressed differently by each individual. It does, however, usually contain elements of quietness and reflection, a simple lifestyle and a journey inwards towards an unidentified goal that will only be recognized when encountered.

While most solitaries will spend periods of time alone, the solitary life nowadays is often experienced within all the excitement of everyday living as it is in our urban family rectory. It seems to me that the key word is *life* and that any devotional practice must inform, and be informed by, daily life. It is an embracing of the whole of life with the whole of the self. Thus solitude, simplicity and silence weave into each day.

I choose to begin the day while the house is still quiet and sit in or look out on to the garden. At present I start by reading a passage from Robert Van de Weyer's *A World Religions Bible* and a page or two from *Quaker Faith and Practice* before reflecting for a while on them and how they engage with each other and my past and present experience. I then move into a time of listening stillness. I do not try to think. It feels like looking through closed eyelids to beyond that place where the butterflies hatch when you are feeling nervous! During this time I hope to deepen my awareness of God. For me this comes as what I can only describe as a reverential sensation of connectedness to all that is. I can say with Gloucester in King Lear: 'I see it feelingly.' Honouring this connectedness leads me to be mindful: that is, trying to be fully present in all I do, noticing the particularity of colours, textures, sounds and relationships with focused attention and being aware of where I engage or withdraw from what I encounter.

Simplicity involves sitting lightly to possessions and I bear in mind the words of William Morris: 'Have nothing in your houses that you do not know to be useful or believe to be beautiful.' I find it somewhat liberating to take a box of no-longer-useful-to-me objects down to the charity shop for someone else to enjoy. But simplicity extends beyond goods to behaviour. It concerns being aware how much self-promotion there is in my conversations, the extravagance of my choices of food and clothes. It covers trying to live sustainably, working for justice – the complications of simplicity are endless! It has also meant that I have had to re-examine my spiritual luggage and lay aside those things that are no longer useful to me in terms of belief or practice. This has the effect of strengthening the truths that remain, which, though fewer, can be held with a steady lightness.

Silence comes in many ways during the day and I find it to be as much an attitude as a physical sensation; perhaps it is better rendered as *stillness*. Even when life is hectic it is possible to have stillness at the core and to work from a clear and sustaining centre. Silence is not of itself necessarily beneficial and there is a world of difference between the atmosphere of a huff and the peace of a quiet evening. It can be an interesting exercise to listen to the positive and negative silences that border our days. Inner silence can be a great friend to the solitary and a companion in queues, waiting rooms and journeys.

For me, the compulsion to explore the solitary life has meant moving away from an established church and joining the Quakers; in some ways an obvious move with their emphasis on simplicity and silent worship. It is also, as I discovered gradually, a very good antidote to the solitary's temptations of inertia and idiosyncrasy!

Anna Botwright

At work

There are those for whom their work is like a prayer – one immediately thinks of a craftsperson or any so-called 'creative' worker. It seems that their work is an expression of who they are and they find God very much in that. If you can identify with that, then enjoy your prayer.

It has not been like that for me. Sometimes work has been a means to an end, a way of paying a mortgage or looking after dependants. I have always worked full-time in human resource management in secular businesses of various sorts, where making a profit is a primary objective. To be honest, that was never so much of a problem in itself. But what can tend to go with it is long hours and uncomfortable commutes, bosses who would have done very well directing those slave galleons, cracking the whip as they shout, 'Faster, faster!', and, to add insult to injury, having given my soul for the good of the firm, the inevitable restructuring and uncertainty about work and pay.

I have found that long hours without much reflection space, feeling driven to do work that was unrewarding, has left me feeling fragmented, disintegrated and exhausted beyond a meaningful prayer life. In addition, particularly in commercial environments, I felt isolated from other people with faith – it was just not talked about.

I certainly don't think I was on my own, though. A colleague recently gave me a cartoon featuring the 'Evil HR Director' being approached by a hapless employee enquiring, 'Are there any company-sponsored programmes for recovery of lost souls – or is it down to the individual?'

If you have responsibilities for others and/or a mortgage to pay it's not so easy and I've struggled for years. First of all you need to notice what's going on. I have used something like the Review of the Day exercise (see Reviewing your life, pages 66–8) to at least acknowledge before God that I felt separated from him and also to help me become more aware of God in the midst of my business, stress and fatigue. This prayer takes only about ten minutes and it's pretty simple, basically becoming aware of God's presence and asking him to show me that for which I am most, also also least, grateful during the day. Tiredness still sometimes overwhelms me and I experiment with doing it at different times of the day. Sometimes I still forget and I just have to get back to it when I remember.

I have also used the Sacred Space website, <www.sacredspace.ie>, in the morning or at least at some time during the day to deliberately bring God into the workspace and particularly into difficult situations. How easy it is to simply forget he's there. Building in reflective space to give my mind a break from endless 'to do' lists has been an important lesson, particularly if I can make the most of commuting journeys with prayer or reading something edifying. I've learnt to recognize that sometimes, more often than I care to admit, the voice shouting 'Faster, faster' and 'Try harder' and 'Not good enough' is my own. I've brought pictures or articles that can remind me of my undernourished spiritual side into the workplace to have something lovely to catch my eye. And when too tired to pray when I get home, simply lighting a candle and allowing the Spirit to intercede stops me from beating myself up because of my lack of a meaningful prayer life. No quick fix, I'm afraid, but if I can't get much prayer space during the week, then it becomes very important to make sure I get some space at other times and particularly when I know I'm going off track.

Anne Strach

Part 4

OVER TO YOU

14

The next steps

We have been delighted and moved by the quality and quantity of the contributions generously made to this book by friends and colleagues. These reflections illustrate what a difference an active relationship with God can make to an individual's life, and yet how personal and particular this difference will be. Our hope is that what you have read here will deepen and enrich your relationship with God in a way that will inevitably change your life too. We hope that your own experience of God has been affirmed and that you have been encouraged to trust it more than you perhaps did before. We hope that you have found some new ways into prayer that might prove helpful, and that you have learnt not to accept your group norms about prayer uncritically. We hope that you have grown in trust in your own ability to see the next steps you need to take to move forward and that you have found a renewed confidence in the God who will both lead and support you as you grow.

Spiritual direction

From time to time through the book we have talked about the value of having a spiritual director, soul friend, spiritual companion, call them what you will. A word about this. Spiritual direction is the art of befriending someone on their spiritual journey. It's a strange term because it isn't just concerned with your *spiritual* journey but with the whole of life, and it isn't concerned with *directing* you in the way we usually understand that word. Get a group of men and women who offer spiritual direction together and one of the things they will all agree on is that 'spiritual direction' isn't the ideal way of describing what they seek to do. The second thing they'll agree on is that they can't all agree on an acceptable alternative! So some stay with the traditional phrase.

Spiritual direction takes place when one person supports and encourages another on their spiritual journey. It can take on all manner of different forms and is dependent upon the relationship between the two people. For many people it will take place in a corporate setting and that will be sufficient for them: worship with others is a form of group spiritual direction. The Methodist 'class system' whereby groups of Christians meet together on a regular basis to share their faith stories and to support each other is another model of group spiritual direction.

Spiritual direction is a gift and most people with some faith experience will exercise this gift a bit sometimes. But there do seem to be some people with a special talent for it. In this sense it's rather like football: just about anybody can kick a ball, even if they fall over doing so, but it takes a rare talent to curve a free-kick like David Beckham. We reckon that 99 per cent of spiritual direction is carried out by ordinary people who have never heard of the term and who have no notion that that is what they are doing. Most groups of people will have among them a person to whom others go for a quiet word of advice on matters of life and faith. For young people it's often a grandparent or favourite aunt or uncle.

Nevertheless it is also a gift that has come to the fore of late. Many Church of England dioceses offer courses in spiritual direction, and they are usually well subscribed. Nearly every diocese these days will also have someone appointed to help people find a spiritual director if they wish to do so. It's a particular ministry that cuts across denominational barriers and is exercised by all manner of folk. Lay people, especially lay women, are much in evidence in its practice.

By now you will, hopefully, have seen how such a ministry might be of help to you. It may be that you already have somebody you talk with in this manner. If you don't then you could consider seeking someone out via the institutional channels of the church.

But you might prefer a more laid-back approach. There is a wise Eastern saying: 'When the pupil is ready the teacher will come.' If God senses that you need a spiritual director then someone will emerge. It may be that they will emerge through the formal channels of the church. But it may be that there is somebody of whom you already know who would be just right. Trust your intuition on this one. If you *had* to go to talk with someone, who would you choose?

Because it is a relationship, it will only work if the chemistry between you is right, and often the only way to find out if that is so is to try it. We suggest that you ask someone if you could meet and talk with them about their offering you this ministry, and that you meet, say, three times to test it out. At the third meeting you can decide if this feels right for you or not. It's not usually anybody's fault if it isn't right, it's more likely to be a matter of 'fitting' or 'not fitting'. If it doesn't fit then seek someone else.

Finding a church

We have tried to offer in this book some insights and resources that might help your spiritual growth. Our aim has been to help you deepen your relationship with the loving God who seeks relationship with each of us. An inevitable potential weakness is that it may encourage a rather individualistic approach to faith. But the God who reaches out to you also reaches out to all humankind, and as the chapter on prayer was at pains to point out, a response to this God involves a changed relationship with everybody else. So part of our faith journey must be corporate in one way or another.

The problem is that it often seems a part of spiritual exploration that much of it has to be undertaken alone, and that all too often the mainline churches don't seem currently to offer much by way of support for such exploration. As people often say: 'I find spiritual direction very helpful. Where might I find a church that would support me in this process?' Where indeed?

Perhaps we shouldn't be too hard on the institutional churches; they are institutions after all, and we must expect them to behave as such. They are good at doing things such as looking after church buildings and necessary church administration, providing regular church services, including the baptizing of babies, taking weddings and burying the dead. Lots of ministers and priests today have time for little else. There is no point in blaming churches for not providing what they can't provide. New life and creativity are rarely found near the centre of any institution.

We need, perhaps, to be more creative and flexible in our relationship with 'church'. For some that will mean getting involved in a major way as members of the church. For others it will mean making a conscious decision to stay on the fringe, worshipping occasionally, but staying clear of institutional involvement. For others again it will mean leaving the mainline churches at least for a time and seeking support elsewhere. Jesus defined church as 'where two or three are gathered together in my name', and maybe some need to look for church along those looser lines: smaller, more creative groups which may have only a short lifespan. Our experience is that there is much more of this creative life about than we imagine: groups of men and women who come together to pray, worship, act in the world and support each other. Sometimes they are present within bigger churches; sometimes they are on the edges or outside of them, but they are there. As they are often small, creative and not always permanent they don't make a lot of noise and may not be very visible. For lots of people Greenbelt is their church; they gather all together only once a year but may meet up in smaller units from time to time. The old models are not the only ones and not necessarily the best ones. The bottom line is to trust that if God wants your faith journey to have a corporate expression then the opportunities for that to happen will be there for you. You just have to spot them and take them!

The next steps, which you may have already started to take, are yours and we wish you well. You will be in our prayers and we hope that we will be in yours. Finally, there is no finally. We could fill more books with 'case studies' and we know that some of you will be able to write your own as you continue to discover new and creative means of responding to God in ways we have not covered or even thought of. We would love to know how you get on. We can be reached at <www.annunciationtrust.org.uk/> where you can also find more resources that might aid your travel.

May God bless you on your journey . . .

Roy Gregory and Henry Morgan

References

G. Appleton, *One Man's Prayers*, London: SPCK, 1967.

Sister Wendy Beckett, *Sister Wendy on Prayer*, London: Continuum, 2006.

Jean Shinoda Bolen, *The Tao of Psychology: Synchronicity and Self*, SanFrancisco: HarperSanFrancisco, 1982.

Common Worship: Daily Prayer, London: Church House Publishing, 2005.

Common Worship: Services and Prayers for the Church of England, London: Church House Publishing, 2000.

A. Dillard, *Pilgrim at Tinker Creek*, New York: Harper Perennial, 1998.

E. Elliot (ed.), *The Journals of Jim Elliot*, Grand Rapids, MI: Revell, 2002.

Exciting Holiness: Collects and Readings for the Festivals and Lesser Festivals of the Church of England, the Church of Ireland, the Scottish Episcopal Church and the Church in Wales, Norwich: Canterbury Press, 2007.

O. H. Frank and M. Pressler, *The Diary of a Young Girl: Anne Frank*, Camberwell, Victoria: Penguin Classics Australia, 1997.

Dag Hammarskjöld, *Markings*, London: Faber and Faber, 1972.

D. Hay, *Exploring Inner Space*, London: Mowbray, 1982.

D. Hay and K. Hunt, *Understanding the Spirituality of People Who Don't Go to Church: A Report on the Findings of the Adults' Spirituality Project at the University of Nottingham*, 2000.

Gerard Manley Hopkins, 'No Worst, There is None. Pitched Past Pitch of Grief'.

E. James, *A Life of Bishop John A. T. Robinson*, London, Collins, 1987.

S. Jeffers, *Feel the Fear and Do It Anyway*, London: Arrow Books, 1991.

R. Johnson, *Inner Work: Using Dream and Active Imagination for Personal Growth*, New York: HarperCollins, 1986.

R. Kamenetz, *The Jew in the Lotus*, New York: HarperOne, 1995.

Christopher Lewis, *Cleave the Wood and There I am: Meditations with Carvings and Music*. Available from Dendron Press, The Old School, Bingfield, Hexham, Northumberland NE46 4HR.

C. S. Lewis, *A Grief Observed*, London: Faber and Faber, 1988.

E. Liebert, *Changing Life Patterns: Adult Development in Spiritual Direction*, Mahwah, NJ: Paulist Press, 1992.

References

A. McCall Smith, *The No. 1 Ladies' Detective Agency*, London: Abacus, 2003.

M. Maxwell and V. Tschudin (eds), *Seeing the Invisible: Modern Religious and Other Transcendent Experiences*, New York: Arkana, 1990.

W. R. Miller (ed.), *The New Christianity*, New York: Delacorte Press, 1967.

H. Morgan (ed.), *Approaches to Prayer*, London: SPCK, 2008.

D. Nicholl, *Holiness*, London: Darton, Longman & Todd, 2004.

Henri Nouwen, *The Genesee Diary*, London: Darton, Longman & Todd, 1995.

J. O'Donohue, *Divine Beauty*, London: Bantam, 2004.

J. O'Donohue, *Eternal Echoes*, London: Bantam, 2000.

L. Osborn, *Paper Pilgrimage*, London: Darton, Longman & Todd, 1990.

Quaker Faith and Practice: The Book of Christian Discipline of the Yearly Meeting of the Religious Society of Friends [Quakers] in Britain, 3rd edn, London: Quaker Books, 2005.

T. Rainer, *The New Diary*, Los Angeles: J.P. Tarcher, 1981.

C. Raymo, *Honey from Stone: A Naturalist's Search for God*, Boston, MA: Cowley, 2005.

R. M. Rilke, *Duino Elegies*, trans. S. Mitchell, London: Picador, 1987.

E. P. Sanders, *The Historical Figure of Jesus*, Harmondsworth: Penguin, 1993.

Mother Teresa, *Come Be My Light: The Private Writings of the Saint of Calcutta*, ed. B. Kolodiejchuk, London: Doubleday, 2007.

A. Tilby, *The Little Office Book*, Berkhamsted: Arthur James, 1998.

E. Underhill, *Practical Mysticism*, London: J. M. Dent, 1914.

R. Van de Weyer, *A World Religions Bible*, Alresford, Hants: O Books, 2003.

J. Walsh (ed.), *The Cloud of Unknowing*, New York: Paulist Press, 1981.